THE DON'T SWEAT GUIDE TO KEEPING YOUR HOME CLEAN

Other books by the editors of Don't Sweat Press

The Don't Sweat Affirmations

The Don't Sweat Guide for Couples

The Don't Sweat Guide for Graduates

The Don't Sweat Guide for Grandparents

The Don't Sweat Guide for Parents

The Don't Sweat Guide for Moms

The Don't Sweat Guide for Weddings

The Don't Sweat Guide to Golf

The Don't Sweat Stories

The Don't Sweat Guide to Travel

The Don't Sweat Guide to Weight Loss

The Don't Sweat Guide to Taxes

The Don't Sweat Guide for Dads

The Don't Sweat Guide to Retirement

The Don't Sweat Guide for Teachers

The Don't Sweat Guide for Newlyweds

The Don't Sweat Guide to Cooking

The Don't Sweat Guide to Your New Home

The Don't Sweat Guide to Holidays

THE DON'T SWEAT GUIDE TO KEEPING YOUR HOME CLEAN

Stop the Clutter from Messing Up Your Peace of Mind

By the Editors of Don't Sweat Press
Foreword by Richard Carlson, Ph.D.

New York

ISBN: 0-7868-8884-9

Hyperion books are available for special promotions and premiums.
For details contact Michael Rentas, Manager, Inventory and Premium Sales,
Hyperion, 77 West 66th Street, 11th floor, New York, New York 10023,
or call 212-456-0133.

FIRST EDITION

10 9 8 7 6 5 4 3 2 1

Contents

Foreword

S omeone once told me that keeping a clean, organized home somehow made it easier to keep a calm, organized mind. I'm not sure if that's always the case, but it sure seems to ring true for me. When my external environment is orderly, I feel better on the inside, as well. I can't quite articulate it, but that's the way it feels.

On the other hand, it's critical that we don't lose perspective about how clean or organized our home happens to be at any given time. It might be important to us, but in the scheme of things, it's still pretty small stuff. In other words, it's not worth sweating over!

In *Don't Sweat the Small Stuff with Your Family,* I included a strategy called "Think of Taking Care of Your Home Like Painting the Bridge." In the chapter, I pointed out that someone once told me that painting the beautiful Golden Gate Bridge in San Francisco was, literally, a full-time job! By the time that workers finish painting the bridge, it's time to start again. In a very real way, that's the way it is with a house or apartment. It's an ongoing process, and once we accept that, it's a lot easier to deal with.

In this book, the editors of Don't Sweat Press have done a wonderful job of balancing the goal of a clean home with the perspective that it's not worth going crazy over! The strategies that you're about to read are simple and based on common sense, but surprisingly effective. My guess is that you're going to receive some insights that will help you achieve a near-perfect balance.

Something that's quite common is for two people who share a home, such as a husband and wife or two roommates, to have very different standards about the importance of a clean and organized home. To one person, something looks like it's perfectly clean, and to another, it appears to be a complete mess! If that sounds familiar, it would be a great idea for both of you to read this book together. You'll find it easier to compromise, see the other person's point of view, and find nice common ground that makes both of you happier and easier to live with.

Whether you live alone or with someone else, I hope you enjoy this book as much as I have, and that it serves you well. Keeping a home clean and organized is a lot more work than meets the eye, and it doesn't always come with a great deal of recognition. I think that after reading this book, however, you'll be a whole lot more relaxed about the process and happier from the inside out.

Treasure yourself, and happy cleaning.

Richard Carlson
Benicia, California, April 2003

THE DON'T SWEAT GUIDE
TO KEEPING YOUR
HOME CLEAN

1.

Know What You Want

If you find yourself consistently frustrated over cleaning your house and keeping it that way, you may want to reconsider the way that you define a clean house. "Clean" means different things to different people, as you probably noted when you walked into a spit-and-polished kitchen with free-range cats eating from the table. Identifying your goals and pinpointing what gets in the way of meeting them can go a long way toward taking the angst out of housecleaning.

Begin by thinking about how you view your house. Is it primarily "home," the place where you can make your nest, find peace, and enjoy family? Is it a "fortress," a bastion against the intrusion of others, the stresses of work, or the noise of society at large? Perhaps it is the stage for entertaining—for hosting outsiders, whether for quiet dinners, community efforts, mother-child play groups, or your teenagers' pals. You may even view it as a work of art, decorated with an eye to visual appeal and aesthetic balance.

Once you have consciously defined what your house is to you, you can think more clearly about just how clean it needs to be. If you're a nester who loves to be home with family and friends around you, you will probably gauge "clean" by what makes everyone feel most at home. If you close the door on the world when you walk through your front door, any considerations of how others will feel about your home become moot—the issue becomes one strictly of what makes you comfortable. If your front door might as well be a revolving one, the idea of having a perfectly clean house at all times should automatically be jettisoned. It won't happen. Heavy household traffic creates dust, dirt, and a changing collection of assorted belongings—yours and others'.

Even if you have a well-formulated idea of what you want your house to be and look like, life is rarely ideal. Decide what you would consider perfect, in terms of clean. Then balance that vision with another that provides the other end of the spectrum. Ask, "What is the absolute minimum of cleanliness I can tolerate?" Most of the time, you can be fairly certain of falling somewhere between the two. At the same time, you can avoid the demon that whispers in your ear, "It can never be clean enough."

2.

Understand the Nature of Dirt

Before you do anything else, shed the notion that you will ever eradicate dirt from your house. Can you cut down on it? Absolutely. Can you get rid of it once and for all? Not on your life.

Dirt is a fact of life. It clings to your shoes in the form of gravel, sand, mud, grass, and soot. It falls from the sky as pollen, pollution, and nature's detritus. It grows in corners and closets as mildew and molds. It emanates from you and others—not to mention your pets. In fact, where there is life, there is also what we think of as "dirt."

Once the truth of dirt's organic and ubiquitous nature is under your belt, you can begin to refine your understanding of dirt. There's "clean" dirt—the good, honest kind that looks beautiful when it knows its place and remains in nature. There's "benign" dirt—the barely visible kind, such as dust that allows the young and insensitive to practice their writing skills on the surfaces of your furniture. There's the more insidious type of dirt—the kind that has a life of its own, grows with neglect, and actually has the potential to cause disease.

Why distinguish one dirt from another? Because certain kinds of dirt really need to be dealt with posthaste. They are the enemies of a wholesome, sweet-smelling, life-sustaining environment. Other kinds of dirt will wait for you to get to them. They may crunch a little underfoot or detract from your view out the window, but they won't kill you. If you let them sit for a week, they won't reproduce on their own.

Based on recent studies, scientists suggest that an overzealous approach to eliminating all dirt actually does us harm. People who constantly wash with disinfecting soaps appear to be more vulnerable to infections. Kids who never keep company with animals—those veritable breeding places of allergens and other debris—actually have a higher incidence of respiratory ailments such as asthma. Further, people who buy and/or overuse many of today's favored cleaners introduce into their environment an array of poisons implicated in cancer, respiratory diseases, and a variety of skin troubles.

Don't turn dirt into an enemy. Understand what it is and what it isn't. Give your first attention to the dangerous stuff, and kick back a little bit more about the rest. You'll get to it sooner or later. You can be sure that it won't go anywhere until you do.

3.

Distinguish Dirt from Clutter

L et's cut to the chase: You'll never be free of dirt. It comes from sources entirely outside of your control. You can only manage it. Clutter, on the other hand, is well within your human capability to control. It may not seem that way—but that's the fact of clutter—humans make it, and humans can choose not to make it.

If you happen to have a high clutter tolerance, good for you. Clutter away. Just keep in mind that your other housecleaning headaches probably relate to your clutter situation. Odds and ends, stacks and piles—all get in the way of such straightforward cleaning components as dusting, mopping, scouring, and vacuuming. As long as the clutter remains, you have two choices. Either you resign yourself to missing a lot of the dirt and dust that you're trying to control, or you double your cleaning time (at least) while you shift the clutter from one spot to another so you can reach the dirt that it shelters.

Maybe you really dislike the mess but have given up hope of ever getting it under control. Perhaps you think that left to your own devices, you could conquer the clutter. The problem, as you see it, is the rest of the people in your household. No matter how much you nag, rag, and wrangle, they refuse to get with the program. As quickly as you put it away, they get it out again.

There's no denying that in an active household, the clutter issue tends to loom large. However, consider the part that you may be playing. For example, have you consciously limited the stuff in your house to what will actually fit in it? In addition, have you made sure that every single belonging of each person in your household actually has a place to go? It's really hard to put something away if there is no "away" to be found. That dresser top may be the only place that your child can find for the two trophies, the seven different-colored hair bands, the curling iron, and the stack of magazines.

Don't let the clutter get you down. Adjust your perspective on the nature of clutter. You are the boss of clutter. You can take control of it and take a big chunk of the work out of housecleaning.

4.

Take Stock

It has often been said that if you aim at nothing, you're sure to hit it. The idea behind this—that to get somewhere, you need to decide where you want to go—applies to housecleaning just as much as it does to so many other aspects of life. The fact that housecleaning gets your goat indicates that something needs to change. That being said, it helps to remember that certain principles dictate how successful you are likely to be at making a change.

For starters, you need to identify why you feel the need to change. Something is irritating you, and the sooner you figure out what it is, the better you will be able to identify its source. Maybe you feel paralyzed. Why? Because the house is such a mess that you feel overwhelmed. Perhaps you feel distracted. Why? Because the clutter that surrounds you prevents you from thinking clearly or working efficiently.

Once you know the why of your desire to change, you also need to pinpoint, in very specific terms, what you would like to change. Whether it's the clutter situation, the lack of help, the need for better tools, or the question of what to do with the exposed rafters in the rustic vault of a ceiling, you need to name the issue. Then figure out what your ideal solution would be. Now you are no longer aiming at nothing. You've got something dead in your sights.

Your next step is how to solve your problem. Instead of bristling under an unidentified feeling of malaise, you've advanced all the way to creating a strategy with a clear goal in mind. It may involve a plan for saving money, finding adequate time, getting the gang to do their part, or any other of dozens of possibilities. It may involve one easy step, or it may require a series of intermediate phases. Either way, if you create a plan, you can get going on whatever needs to happen first.

If you've been flummoxed until now, try a simple exercise. Take a blank piece of paper and print in large capital letters at the top: "THIS HAS GOT TO CHANGE!" Then write out the following questions, leaving room after each for your answers.

1. Why do I feel the need for change?
2. What specifically is wrong?
3. What would be ideal?
4. How can I make such a change happen?

Your answer to the final question should list one or more specific actions that you can take and then check off.

Change can be a challenge, but don't turn it into a monster for lack of facing and tackling it. Start small. Be persistent. Take pride. Even housecleaning can be conquered.

5.

Evaluate Your Time Commitments

Do you feel as though you never have enough time to clean your house properly? Well, guess what? That may not be only a feeling. It may be the reality. There are at least three ways to skin this issue of too little time.

One, find a way to free up more of your discretionary time and apply it to housecleaning—less television time, less elaborate food preparation, less retail therapy, and so on. Your time commitments are yours to make. You have choices. Granted, living responsibly and humanely will make some commitments obvious and unavoidable. Others are genuinely negotiable. Give real consideration to whether adjusting the way that you "spend" some of your time might just clear the decks for more satisfying housecleaning.

Two, find as many ways as possible to make cleaning more efficient, and therefore, less time-consuming. This may require updated tools, a better system, more mini-cleans that take a few minutes a day, or some more effective methods. It's easy to spin your wheels. Individuals have successfully devoted entire careers to finding ways to improve performance on virtually every job in existence. It can be done. You can do it with housecleaning.

Three, pay someone to do some or all of the work for you. If you work outside your home, you should have an approximate idea of what your working hours are worth. Compare the commercial value of your time with what you would have to pay someone to clean for you. If you're paid at least as much for your time as you would pay someone for an equal amount of cleaning time, it may be worth considering. Remember, it's not all or nothing. You can have occasional help: every other week, just the windows, spring and fall cleanings, or anything in the middle.

The point is this: You have only so many hours in a day and only so many days in a lifetime. Consider your commitments. Change them if need be. Choose how you use your time.

6.

Suit Your Goals to Your Household

By now, you have an ideal in mind when you think of getting your housecleaning under control. The question is, how realistic is that ideal in relation to your household, the people with whom you share your house, your phase of life, and the sorts of activities that typically take place in your home? There's no point in setting a benchmark that will never be attainable. To create an impossible goal only increases your frustration and discouragement.

First of all, what about your house? Is it large and rambling? A compact condo? An antique? A shore house? The size and environment of your house will determine how easy it is to keep it clean. The issue of acreage alone can make an enormous difference, as can the amount of mud, sand, gravel, or other loose matter immediately outside your doors.

In a fourteen-room Victorian, expecting to thoroughly clean the entire house in one morning every week is expecting too much. You might more realistically plan to give the heavy-traffic area on the first floor and all the bathrooms a thorough cleaning every week, and add a quick touch-up with the broom or vacuum midweek. The upstairs can alternate from week to week between a heavy clean and a light one. In a small place, it may be completely reasonable to expect that you'll go over every surface weekly. A small place actually accumulates dirt more comprehensively than a large place because the entire dwelling sees heavy traffic all the time. However, because you have fewer square feet to cover, you don't need a lot of time to clean it.

The size, age, and extent of the family living in your home also have an impact on cleaning. If you're in the midst of raising four kids, you'd be foolish to expect the kind of order and cleanliness that a retired couple might expect. Rather, you'd show admirable home-management ability if you could aim to have the clutter clear by bedtime each night and a weekly shedding of the past week's grime.

Give yourself a break as you set your goals. Make as honest an assessment of your home situation as you can. Be thankful for what you have and the stage of life that you're enjoying. A household of growing children is notoriously busy and messy—but precious. A home that shelters one or two is relatively quiet and under control—and golden. Once you've assessed, let your goals reflect the truth about your household. Let go of expectations that can only lead to fretting.

7.

Create a Plan

L ike any project, housecleaning benefits from some forethought and strategizing. Once you have reckoned with what you have, where you are in life, and what you want, you can begin to spell out for yourself exactly what it will take to get your house in order.

Start by putting the various cleaning jobs, from dusting and vacuuming to cleaning drapes and changing filters, into categories. Most obvious of the categories is how often a job needs to be done. This is subjective, of course. Some people may want to dust once or twice a week. Others may see every crumb and piece of lint on carpets and floors, making frequent vacuuming a must. Certainly, the big jobs that fall within a traditional "spring cleaning" category can readily go on the list for once- or twice-a-year jobs. Just naming the jobs will help you begin to cut the housecleaning monster down to size. Deciding how often they must be done will shrink it even further.

Keep in mind that one of your goals is to take some of the toil out of your housework. Err on the side of not cleaning quite often enough, at first, and see if more often is really as important as you're inclined to think. You may have created "needs," in theory, that turn out, in fact, to be overkill. Right now, take it easy, and see what small corrections accomplish before you get carried away.

Now look at your calendar for the coming year. Consider realistically when the big jobs will fit in to your life. For example, planning to redo your closets in March, during your children's spring vacation when you typically travel as a family, will probably set you up for failure. Be honest with yourself. Find your time slots, make your plan, and schedule your big housecleaning jobs on the calendar in exactly the way that you schedule getaways and appointments.

Look for jobs that need to happen quarterly and monthly, as well. These may not need a specific date on the calendar as much as a certain week or month. "At the end of June and December, I turn the mattress." "At some point in the last week of each month, I clean the inside of the refrigerator." Just giving yourself an approximate deadline on the calendar will allow you to clear your mind of the details without stress.

For the weekly and more frequent jobs, your biggest challenge will be to discover what works. Make a plan. Try it out. If it doesn't serve, rethink it, and make a change. Housecleaning does not have to hang over your head like a dark, heavy cloud. Put the plan on paper, follow it, and lighten the mental load.

8.

Be Flexible

Once you have a plan for your housekeeping, prepare yourself for the fact that real life will certainly sometimes get in the way. What will you do when it does? Whatever you do, don't fall into the "all-or-nothing" trap. Because you can't meet a deadline doesn't mean that you abandon the job altogether. Because you can't finish the whole job doesn't mean that you can't do some portion of it.

As with the overall picture of housecleaning, you can give yourself a boost in advance by planning your contingencies. If you must shorten your weekly cleaning for some reason, what will you allow to wait? What are your "must-do" items? How might you divide the work into two or three shorter sessions? If something comes up that makes a routine quarterly or yearly cleaning job impossible, what is the earliest time that it can be rescheduled? Is this an instance in which it might be feasible and/or wise to hire someone to do it for you?

This may sound like cleaning overkill. Not at all. Far from overemphasizing the importance of getting the job done, having a plan for needed schedule changes helps to prevent several of the most stressful aspects of housecleaning. First, it ensures that the cleaning doesn't back up in such a way that you find yourself with an overwhelming (or embarrassing) mess to dig out of. Second, it reduces the fret factor associated with the unexpected. Instead of settling into a quiet, discomfiting stew when plans go awry, you can simply put your alternative plan on the calendar and get on with the business at hand. Finally, it affords you a good measure of satisfaction and self-esteem.

Flexibility is one of the most underrated of life's skills. In all arenas of life, flexibility helps you keep your balance, maintain your sense of humor, and put relationships and challenges in perspective. You can turn a potential pitfall into a great tutorial in flexibility. Do it faithfully, and you'll find that your ability to bend and stretch in other aspects of your life increases, too.

9.

Be Realistic

Making a major change in your housecleaning habits may seem daunting to you. After all, your current habits developed for specific reasons. They have to do with your upbringing, your temperament, your energy level, and your lifestyle. Whether or not you like the way that you handle housecleaning at the moment, you're used to doing things the way that you do them. That puts those habits in your "comfort zone," and your comfort zone can be a briar patch to climb out of.

After you've made a plan for your ideal cleaning schedule, look at how much change it actually represents. There's no question; habits of all sorts, including housecleaning, can be made and they can be broken. The change that you've outlined is absolutely doable. However, depending on how radically different it is from your present experience, it may take time to get used to your new habits.

Consider taking on your new housecleaning plan step by step. Break the changes down into component parts. For example, it may be enough for the next month simply to maintain a daily practice of putting away clothes and clutter before going to bed. You'll be amazed, if that's one of your problem areas, what a transformation such a commitment can make in your overall housecleaning. Without the surface mess, the basic cleaning moves one hundred percent more quickly. Perhaps you can dedicate the next month to making sure that you accomplish at least a rudimentary dust, vacuum, and scour routine once a week—while maintaining the de-clutter habit, of course. From there, you can move on to prompt laundry folding, then on to monthly woodwork polishing.

If you look at what you want to accomplish as a whole regimen, it may have the rough outline of Mount Everest. Treat your psyche with some respect. Be realistic about the time that it takes to actually break old habits and make new ones. Create paths, plateaus, and scenic overviews along the way. Your changes will be both manageable and lasting.

10.

Look at the Bright Side

For many people who are discouraged over housecleaning, the word "dread" seems to pop up often. They dread the mess that they face. They dread the tedium of what cleaning entails. They dread the prospect of no sooner being finished than needing to begin again.

If dread is part of your housecleaning vocabulary, maybe it's time to expand your vocabulary. Keep in mind that language exerts a powerful influence over us all. The words that we choose affect our moods, perspective, and attitudes. They define reality as we experience it, because they focus our attention in a certain direction. If we use negative language in relation to housecleaning, we shift our focus to what bothers us most about it. It becomes drudgery, pain, and something to avoid.

Imagine instead that you replace "dread," and all of the negatives that are its partners, with "look forward to." That expression, "look forward to," carries a load of hope and cheer. Instead of focusing on what you dislike, it anticipates a happy prospect. "I look forward to making that tabletop gleam. The grain in the wood is gorgeous when it's well polished," "I look forward to putting a big bouquet of red tulips in front of that mirror after I've cleaned it," or, "I look forward to sitting down in this room and feeling like I can really rest." You can look forward to aspects of the process. You can look forward to the outcomes. Either way, you've shifted your focus toward the bright side.

Consider what housecleaning gives you as a reward for your effort. Even take the time to make a list. Like a successful dieter who focuses on "getting fit" instead of "losing weight," think about what you gain in the process of cleaning instead of what you lose. It may be a beautiful environment, an end to a lost-and-found lifestyle, freedom to invite friends in, or simply personal satisfaction. Whatever it is, you have it because you exerted the time and effort in housecleaning. Make each positive aspect of cleaning a gift to yourself. Remember it. Rehearse it. Look forward with pleasure and satisfaction.

11.

Make a Place for Everything

The principle of "a place for everything" addresses several typical scenarios that get in the way of efficient cleaning. First, there's the overload situation. The average American home is overloaded with things. We are a consumer society, and under the influence of highly sophisticated and successful advertising campaigns, we buy far more than we need or could ever use in a lifetime. Typically, the latest purchases push previous purchases into the backs of closets, basements, attics, and garages. Over time, those storage areas fill up and overflow. Then "clean the garage (hall closet, basement, and so on)" becomes the monster item on the "to do" list, while the new purchases become visible clutter that can't be remedied.

Another challenge to "a place for everything" is the issue of organization. Because belongings tend to come into a household in a relatively organic manner—bit by bit, so to speak—they often get put away in an equally unregulated way. They land in whatever space is available at the moment, which is to say that they have no designated home when they are not in use. What does this mean? Usually it means that such items stay out in view and move from one surface or corner to another.

Even when you've done the essential job of creating a place for something, you can run into trouble if the place doesn't make sense. For example, storing all of your cleaning supplies in the hall closet, when some of those supplies see daily use in other places—kitchen, bathrooms, family room—can really subvert your best efforts at tidiness. So, too, can assigning such items as bulky sweaters or jeans to an under-the-bed bin that is hard to get at. The sheer inconvenience of your storage choice easily leads to items simply being left where they were last used.

Making a place for everything requires forethought and self-discipline: forethought in terms of what you will store where and how; self-discipline in terms of knowing the actual storage capacity of your home and honoring it. You can keep your house relatively free of clutter only if the items have somewhere to go. The more logical and convenient that "somewhere" is, the more likely it is that you'll use it. If you are conscientious about limiting what you own, it will be easier for you to put your belongings where they belong.

12.

Eliminate Excess

It's all very well to agree that most of us own too many things. It's another matter to do something about it—but don't despair. You can do something about the excess in your home, and once you get the hang of it, you may even learn to enjoy it.

Start small and work your way up to bigger, more challenging items. For example, how many half-used health and beauty items are you storing in your linen closet and bathroom? Maybe you experimented and found that you didn't like what you tried. You may feel as though it's a "waste" to throw away a perfectly good half-bottle of that so-so shampoo. Well, guess what? It's a waste of your valuable storage space to keep it. Either throw the bottle in the trash or find someone to whom you can pass it along. Old or unused supplies need a new life or disposal. It's as simple as that. If they've sat in your closet unused for a year, you're never going to use them. So get rid of them.

Think in similar terms about clothing that you keep bringing out in season but never wear. Don't fool yourself into thinking that the time may come when you want to wear those clothes. Whether you remember why or not, you do have a reason for never getting around to wearing them. Share your wealth. Give those clothes to someone who really needs or likes them. Numerous charities distribute donated clothes. You only have to deposit them in a clothing drop box. In the case of clothes that are next to new and simply not for you, you may have a friend or family member for whom they would be just the thing to brighten up a ho-hum wardrobe. Recycle those clothes, and free your storage for what you'll really wear.

The same can be said for books, furnishings, outgrown children's items, old magazines, toys, sports equipment, lawn tools, and so on. Anything that sits in your house unused or disliked, season after season, should be released from captivity, once and for all. Practice ruthless honesty with yourself about what makes you hold on to things that have outlived their usefulness to you. Then part with them happily, and enjoy your lightened load.

13.

Make Sense of Storage

Once you've eliminated what you don't want or need, there still remains the job of putting what you keep in order. The better organized and more efficient your storage is, the more likely you are to use it and keep it in good order.

Begin by assessing the storage that you have. Consider the location of each storage space, its capacity, and whether you have found the best way to use it to the utmost. Then consider how and when you use the various items that you need to store. The closer your storage is to where you use the item that you're storing, the easier it will be to put the item away when you're through with it.

Next, think about how best to create storage "centers" for certain categories of goods. For example, if possible, you may want to create a closet or space in a garage in which you can put all of your sports equipment. Since such equipment tends to get outdoor use (which means that it can hold outdoor dirt), you take advantage of location logic when you store it in a place that is on your way "out." You also eliminate one of the sources of tracked dirt. You can create similar storage centers for cleaning supplies, hobby supplies, seasonal clothes, indoor games and videos/DVDs, reference books, collections, important papers and financial records, and so forth.

Once you've categorized items for storage and found good locations to put them, organize the space itself. It helps to know what you're storing before you decide how you want to make the storage efficient. Once you've matched space to goods, you can take advantage of a wide range of inexpensive shelving, hooks, containers, and racks to put things away in a neat, accessible way.

It takes some thought and time to make the most of the storage that you have, but it's well worth the investment. With care and planning, you'll not only have a place for everything, you'll be excited about using it.

14.

Cycle and Recycle

You don't have to let your material possessions take over your living space. You simply need to get into the swing of moving material out of your house as regularly as it moves in.

Prime targets for the recycling process arrive daily in the mail or on your doorstep—magazines, newspapers, junk mail, catalogs, and other mail. Believe it or not, this is the easy stuff, since most communities now mandate recycling. You can stay on top of the "in-box" component of your home by making a point of looking at your mail right away. Immediately toss anything that you're not interested in. Put important mail in the place that you've designated for it, to be handled at your regular time. Anything that you can't decide about, put in a special bin for just that category of mail. Let it sit for a maximum of a week. That's plenty of time to make up your mind. You'll either act on it or toss it.

Periodicals and daily newspapers should likewise receive prompt attention. When the morning paper arrives, put yesterday's edition in the recycling bin. Better yet, put today's there as soon as you're done reading it. When a monthly or weekly magazine arrives, recycle the previous week's or month's issue. If, for some reason, you want to save a particular article, clip it and file it. If you like to keep back copies for a period of time, that's fine. Just put a real limit on how many—one year, six months, or whatever.

Likewise, make a weekly date with yourself to rummage through the refrigerator. Anything that has sat for a week in there should be examined, smelled, and reconsidered. It's no more wasteful to throw out aging food than it is to let it take up space while it turns into a science experiment. Freezer items should be tossed after six to twelve months, depending on the particular item. This is true of pantry items, too. A year is long enough for most foodstuffs. Use it or lose it.

You also have a finite amount of closet and drawer space for clothes. Don't buy new clothes until you're prepared to discard some of the old. You can make it a one-for-one operation. A new sweater? Which one am I replacing?

The cycle and recycle process can apply to anything that you simply don't want, need, or like. It's amazing how much more easily you can clean a room that isn't loaded with unnecessary or unattractive furniture. Outlets for used furniture abound. You can either be generous with a donation or actually pull in some petty cash through a consignment or garage sale.

Consider this the physics of housecleaning: For each item that comes in, one needs to go out. If you maintain the basic in-out balance, you can help to keep your balance as housecleaner.

15.

Be Green

M any of the cleaning chemicals on the market today have the potential to add up to disastrous pollutants. The good news is that several simple changes can put you on the "green" team of individuals today who are committed to living in a kinder, gentler relationship to the Earth. You don't have to give up cleanliness. You don't have to boycott all but the one hundred percent "natural" products. You do need to use cleaning products in a thoughtful, informed way.

Begin by cutting back on the number of products that you use. Remember that the biggest reason manufacturers produce so many "specialized" products is to keep you buying. You'll save yourself a lot of confusion, storage trouble, and chemical contamination by choosing one or two basic products to do all of the jobs in the house. A good all-purpose cleaner goes a long way toward effectively cleaning most items. In fact, you can look on the Internet or in a local natural food store for some environment-friendly cleaners that you mix up as you need them in concentrations appropriate for the job at hand.

Cut back, as well, on the amount of cleaner that you use as you go. Instead of applying a liberal coat of cleaner to a surface, apply it to the cleaning tool. It will be more effective and greatly reduce the amount of solution you use. You will find that you can also cut down on the amount of cleaner by giving it a little time to work. (Have you noticed that dishes and pans that have been soaked don't need as much cleanser or elbow grease?)

Remember, too, that good tools can cut down on what cleaning solutions you need. Keep your cleaning tools in good repair and replace them as soon as they need it. Take advantage of squeegees, non-damaging scrubbers, reusable cloths, and non-power floor tools. You'll save electricity, water, and raw materials.

Most of all, stay on top of your cleaning so that the jobs don't become dramatic. Wiping up the kitchen and bathroom daily means that you don't have buildup to contend with. Promptly spot-cleaning carpets and furniture after spills or staining means that you don't need harsh measures to get the spots out. Using the least possible amount of cleaners means that you don't have to remove the buildup at some later time. Be a thoughtful cleaner. The planet will thank you.

16.

Create a De-clutter Routine

If you're a normal American, you've probably developed some habits that you wouldn't dream of changing. You shower once a day. You brush your teeth morning and evening. You typically eat three meals a day. You pick up your daily mail (or e-mail, if you're wired). You probably give these habits little to no thought; they're givens in your daily routine, repeated to the point of doing them on autopilot.

Well, here's another item to put on the "auto" list. Once a day, pick up the clutter throughout the house. Many people find it most effective to do this before bed, when the day's activities (and cluttering) have ended. That way, you have a guaranteed six to eight hours of neatness, albeit while you're asleep, before the clutter begins to pile up again. Others prefer to put everything in order after morning ablutions but before the workday begins. In that case, the house is ready for unexpected visitors, straightened up for whatever you hope to accomplish for the day, or simply a pleasant setting for relaxation.

A daily pickup drastically reduces the amount of clutter that can accumulate. One day's pileup cannot compare to the debris of a week or more. The lack of clutter also makes every other housecleaning job easier. You'll waste less time looking for items that could be buried under an ever-growing load of stuff. Instead, they are in their rightful places at least once a day.

Of course, you may find that once you establish a daily de-clutter routine, you actually learn to make less clutter in the first place. Most clutter happens because someone has procrastinated. Someone used something, then left it where it was instead of putting it away. With practice, you can learn to put things away in a timely manner. With few exceptions—those being jobs or pastimes that require a temporary mess—you can avoid the whole clutter problem in the first place.

17.

Share the Load

A lack of cooperation can certainly subvert the best intentions and actions of the dedicated housecleaner. Rather than let it become an issue for family warfare, work for positive house-wide change. Begin by communicating what you hope to accomplish— that is, a daily de-clutter. Explain that with each person taking responsibility only for his or her own mess, no one gets stuck with a big or unfair amount of work. Then suggest a plan for how to de-clutter daily.

If you have small children, you have a job to do, but it will pay big dividends. Teaching each child to clean up after him- or herself is giving that child a wonderful tool for life. You need to be consistent and disciplined in making sure that each child does the job. You need to spell out consequences in the case of refusal (for example, the toys or clothes that they leave out get put in storage for a period of time). Children actually rise to the occasion of a consistent lesson, so it's well worth the effort.

If you have older children who have been allowed to leave their messes to someone else, you have more of an uphill battle, but it isn't impossible. Appeal to their sense of fairness—most young people have an ample supply. Explain that your time is just as important to you as theirs is to them. Someone has to clean up the mess, and it shouldn't be you, if you didn't make it. You may decide to let them make their own rules for their own rooms. If you're comfortable with that, simply insist that everything they own must end up in their own rooms by the end of each day. Anything that they took out that is common property must be put where it belongs as soon as they're through with it. Then close the doors on the messes that they keep in their rooms.

A clutter-prone spouse is probably the most problematic family member to deal with. It's the rare adult who appreciates being "taught" by his or her spouse. Again, communication is key. Rather than making clutter the stuff of battles, make it a topic of friendly conversation. Explain what bothers you and why. Suggest reasonable solutions that you can work on together. Go so far as to provide a basket, cupboard, or even a room that your spouse can treat as he or she pleases. Concentrate your efforts on public and common spaces, and let the good effects of neatness expand organically.

It's not unreasonable to ask for some cooperation in making your home the kind of place in which you can relax and enjoy yourself and others. Be the ambassador of de-cluttering. You don't have to go it alone.

18.

Lose the Shoes

S hoes are responsible for a lot of tracked dirt and not a few minor trip-ups and stubbed toes. What to do? Put those shoes in their place.

First of all, outdoor shoes are designed for outdoors. It's no wonder that they become such purveyors of outside dirt and grime. At a minimum, you will do yourself a great favor by installing high-quality doormats, both outside and inside every door of your house, and reminding your household members to use them. You can confine a lot of dirt to the doorstep by doing so. You'll make the mats even more effective if you remember to sweep, vacuum, or shake them every day or as needed. Once they're loaded with dirt, they become as much of a problem as a solution.

Consider, as well, the possibility of providing a place at each door where people can remove their outdoor shoes and leave them. There are countries in which a person would not dream of wearing outdoor shoes beyond the threshold. In your home, you have the right to make such a custom your own. You'll probably want to make sure that each family member has "indoor" shoes to put on, for warmth, comfort, and safety. If you intend for visitors to abide by your shoeless custom, it would be a courtesy to warn them and encourage them to bring slippers, socks, or sandals. You can also make the outdoor/indoor switch strictly a family matter. In any case, the less outdoor traffic you have, the better contained the outdoor dirt will be.

Remember that shoes, like other household items, become clutter if you don't create a space for them. If you decide to leave shoes at the door, provide a closet, shelf, or rack on which they can be neatly stored. Do the same for the shoes that serve as indoor shoes. You'll readily find shoe racks for doors, closet floors, or walls in any home goods store or catalog. They don't cost much in dollars or effort, but they save a lot in floor clutter.

19.

Maintain Filters

One of the dandy innovations of modern times is the filter. Virtually any appliance or heating system that pushes or pulls air comes equipped these days with a filter. Forced-air heating systems, air conditioners, vacuum cleaners, vents in kitchens and bathrooms, and windows all have their own versions of filters. The filter serves to catch airborne particles such as lint, dust, pollen, and grease, or to prevent the passage of small bodies (such as insects). This means that fewer of these particles and creatures are loose in your environment, settling into furnishings and onto surfaces.

Filters are your friends until you neglect them. As they collect the particles in the passing air, they become less effective. They may eventually restrict air passage, preventing the efficient operation of the machine that they are supposed to serve—sometimes even causing damage to the machine. Alternatively, they may become a source of the very particles that they are supposed to filter. When their holding capacity is breached, the force of the air blowing through them may push the filtered bodies back into your environment.

Do yourself a favor. Locate the filter on every air system that operates in your home. Read owner's manuals or call manufacturers to find out where to purchase and how to change replaceable filters, how to clean nondisposable filters, and how often each filter needs such care. Create a tag or chart to attach to each given filter to keep track of when you need to clean or change it.

Just this simple maintenance can save you incalculable expense and time in both keeping your house clean and keeping your modern conveniences in good repair. This is a classic case of a stitch in time. It's easy when it's timely.

20.

Do-It-Once Laundry

A s with all other household cleaning jobs, your laundry needs are specific to your own household. You can eliminate one or more steps in the laundry process with some forethought and customizing of your laundry routine.

For example, a growing number of homes locate the laundry room in the same area as the bedrooms, which is to say, where the dirty wash is made. If that's your situation, consider making space for dirty laundry right where your washer is. If you have the room, line up or stack several baskets on shelves. Label them "whites," "lights," "darks," and "delicates." Let each household member bring his or her dirty clothes directly to "Laundry Central" and do the sorting on the spot.

Suppose that you either lack the space by the washer or have the old traditional laundry-in-the-basement setup. You may want to aim for a modification of the sort-as-you-go plan. Laundry bags on frames are easy to come by in home goods stores and catalogs and department stores. Even better, you can purchase a laundry bag on a frame that is equipped with two bins. This allows the user to make at least a preliminary sort of darks and lights. Provide each bedroom or bathroom in your household with one of these. On a designated day of the week, have the individual who uses the bag deposit it in the laundry room. Remember, even very small children can be taught to sort. It's one of the first skills that they'll be tested on and encouraged to improve in school. In fact, you can make a learning game of it that helps both you and the kids.

Once you have your household laundry in one place with a rough sort already done, your job is much simplified. The two scenarios above can be modified in any number of ways, depending on the age and number of people in your household. It's another situation in which a small investment of thought, equipment, and cooperation can save you time and effort. You may even find that your household members become more invested in the process of keeping house as they assume this responsibility.

21.

Choose Quality Tools

Perhaps the tools that we use in the privacy of our own homes don't have the sex appeal of a car, a piece of apparel, or a piece of sports equipment. However, they see at least as much use over many years and exert a profound effect on our ability to work efficiently and with enjoyment. So why do so many people buy cheap, hold on to cleaning tools long after they're shot, or make do with less than the optimum?

Surely, one of the best ways to make cleaning less of a chore is to use the best-quality tools that you can afford and keep those tools in good repair. An old or inadequate vacuum means going over the same acreage several times every cleaning day, because the machine simply doesn't pick everything up the first time. A worn-out mop means that even after you wash the floor, you need to get down on all fours to clean the spots that the mop didn't touch.

Take a look at your collection of tools. When was the last time that you serviced or replaced the vacuum? How up-to-date are the brushes, cloths, sponges, and dusting wand? Does the mop head need attention? Are the rubber edges on the squeegee and dustpan in good repair? Do you have the most efficient tools for the particularities of your home?

Cleaning tools may not top your list of fun items for which to shop, but it's worth every minute of your attention to find the best and make them part of your cleaning arsenal. The truth is that you actually do get what you pay for. Quality tools from a good hardware store or janitorial supply house usually cost more than the cheap substitutes available in the bargain aisle of the supermarket—with good reason. They are made from higher-quality materials and better designed for the work at hand. In the long run, you probably come out ahead on the cost. That higher-priced, quality equipment has a longer life expectancy, takes some of the drudgery out of the job, and saves you a significant amount of time whenever you use it.

Don't be seduced by the latest come-on or the deepest price cuts. Do a little research on the tools you need, and then choose what you will buy according to what will do the job best. Compare prices from one retail outlet to another, keeping in mind that the same good brand names will sometimes show up in the discount stores at reduced prices. Then treat yourself to the pleasure and efficiency that those tools offer.

22.

Consolidate Supplies

A sk yourself this question: Do you know exactly where all of your cleaning supplies are every time that you need them? If your answer is yes, you're ahead of the game. Many people have supplies scattered here and there, often left in the places that they were last used. When cleaning day or a spot job arises, valuable time and energy end up being wasted on the hunt for the appropriate tools and materials.

The solution requires a once-and-for-all consideration of what you use, how often you use it, and where it is most often used. Once you've figured your cleaning habits into the mix, you can arrange all of your cleaning supplies so you never have to hunt again.

Start with the supplies that you use less often—waxes and polishes, carpet shampoo, window equipment, and other once-in-a-while materials. These are prime candidates for a "janitor's closet." If you're lucky enough to actually have a utility room or closet, this makes a perfect location for your cleaning materials. Once you've found an efficient way of storing supplies in this spot, your greatest challenge will be simply to make sure that you keep only those supplies that you actually use. Toss anything that is past its prime or not to your liking. Keep the rest stored in such a way that you can see everything at a glance. This holds true for the supplies that you need in the basement or garage of your house, as well.

In short, you want to whittle down the supplies that you have to what you actually use; you want to create a central place for the big and broadly applied indoor supplies and tools; and you want to make accessible storage for the garage- and basement-specific tools and cleaners. Take a trip to one of your local superstores and take advantage of the many shop-style organizers. Hang, stack, and arrange your supplies in such a way that it's a pleasure to find them, use them, and put them away.

23.

Store It Where You Use It

For supplies that are used more than once a week—in the kitchen and bathrooms, for example—you'll save yourself a lot of steps by keeping a full stock in each location. There's no harm and a lot of efficiency in duplicating any small equipment (sponges, brushes, squeegees) and supplies (all-purpose cleaner, disinfectant, bleach) that you routinely use in those high-maintenance locations. You don't want to trek to the utility closet every time that you want to wipe down the counter or scour the sink.

Purchase an under-the-counter supply caddy that can efficiently hold the supplies for each specific location. These are readily available in supermarkets, department stores, hardware stores, and janitorial supply outlets. Caddies will help to prevent storage clutter. The caddy, by virtue of its design, keeps things neat, accessible, and confined to a prescribed amount of space. Again, keep only the supplies that you actually use. Anything else will only take up valuable space and make it harder to access the supplies that you use all the time.

Pay attention to the location of replacement parts, as well. Mops need new sponges or heads from time to time. Vacuums need new filters and bags. Keep such parts in the same place that you store the items that they supply. It's one more way to take the guesswork out of where to find the supply when you need it. You'll also reduce the excess by making all of your supplies readily visible and countable.

Buy replacement supplies as soon as you open a backup that you've stored. That way, you'll never find yourself short in the midst of a cleaning job. By thinking through what you need, having a clear view of what you have, and storing supplies where you use them, you'll eliminate much of the labor from your cleaning routine.

24.
Think Small

Half of the challenge facing anyone who wants to make housecleaning less of a chore and more of a joy is attitude. As with so many other aspects of life, the thoughts and emotions that you associate with housecleaning will largely determine your ability to do it with a smile. The more negativity that you load onto housecleaning, the bigger and more dreadful the job grows in your estimation. What is essentially a collection of minor routines, many of which need to be done only periodically, swells to ogre-like proportions.

You can change your habits of thought just as certainly as your habits of activity. Begin by adjusting your view of what it means to clean. If you are someone who gets a kick out of experiencing dramatic transformations, then you may enjoy letting a week's worth of dirt and clutter accumulate so that your once-a-week cleaning makes a visibly dramatic difference. If, on the other hand, the overall job of housecleaning looms large, week after week, you may find that you need to break it into smaller parts.

There's no reason, for example, why you have to clean bathrooms on the same day that you dust. Vacuuming upstairs can be done on a different day than vacuuming downstairs. A once-a-day thorough wiping of kitchen counters and what's on them can make that job a non-item on the weekly list. It may be that giving one hour a day to various smaller jobs—dusting a room, spot-cleaning around doorknobs or light switches—will mean that the big job takes half as long. By the time that you're finished, you may whittle down what you consider "big" jobs to a couple of times a year.

Now consider housecleaning in the context of your life and times. Is there any sense in which you make too much of the business of cleaning? Does it warrant the time, energy, and fuss that you invest in it? If you did less or overlooked a few details from time to time, would anyone suffer as a result? Would anyone other than you even notice?

Housecleaning is a worthy job, and finding ways to make it more efficient and effective can certainly add quality to your life. When your attitude toward housecleaning actually brings you down, however, it's time to reassess. Lay this work alongside qualities such as health, friendship, peace, and compassion, and see whether the business of housecleaning seems like quite so big a deal.

25.

Do It Now

Negativity isn't the only thing that makes housecleaning harder. Procrastination can cause just as much anxiety and irritability as a bad attitude can. Once you've taken active notice of a housekeeping job that needs to be done, putting it off can only serve to put a nagging voice in your ear and a feeling of self-recrimination in your heart.

Do yourself a favor. When you see something that ought to be done, take action. Don't waste precious time and energy fretting over it. Get busy and either do the job now, or make a specific plan with a timetable for getting it done as soon as possible.

If the job requires multiple steps or stages, list the steps in order, and start doing what is needed to check each item off. Perhaps you have to call someone whose help you need. Maybe a trip to a hardware store is called for to purchase some supply or other. Maybe the job requires that some other job be accomplished first. You'll be surprised at how rewarding it can be simply to make a start.

On a more philosophical level, consider what it is that makes you put off jobs that you know you could do now. Procrastinators tend to act consistently over the full range of their lives. They put off actions on all fronts. The net result is a constant sense of "more to do," which robs them of peace and relaxation. It's worth some reflection to sort out what you achieve by refusing to act now instead of later. If you can say with conviction that you achieve nothing by your procrastination, you have a building block for changing your behavior to a more constructive pattern.

Whether or not you get to the bottom of your procrastination habit, though, you can change the behavior. Why bother? First, you relieve the mental strain of procrastination. Second, you handle jobs while they're still small, instead of putting them off until they become big, labor-intensive jobs. Ironing a few items fresh out of the dryer is a whole lot less work than dealing with a basketful of cold, rumpled laundry that has been piling up for a week or more. Swiping over the drip pans on the stove after every use is a lot easier than scrubbing the cooked-on splatters of many days.

Granted, there are cleaning jobs that can wait. Just realize that if you have a job on your mind and you're putting it off, you're carrying extra mental baggage. If you want a more carefree housecleaning experience, you'll act promptly when a job calls.

26.

Don't Stop at the Door

Even with the best indoor doormats that money can buy and a solid, no-shoe policy within your four walls for family and friends, outdoor dirt will find its way into your house. You can't eliminate it altogether—that's understood. However, you can push it back a little farther by taking your cleaning routines beyond the thresholds of your household entrances.

Let's assume that you make it a regular habit to vacuum or shake out the rugs that usually lie inside each door. By doing so, you make the most of their holding potential and prevent as much indoor tracking of outdoor dirt as you can. Your next preventive step should take you out the door.

Apartments and condominiums with doors that open onto an interior hallway will automatically help you keep the great outdoors where it belongs. Yet you can still stand a buffer from the free-ranging grit and dust that accumulate in public hallways. Find a good mat with a rubber or vinyl backing. This will prevent trips and falls and allow you to wipe your feet without the rug moving.

If you have an entryway or porch outside your door, you still need a good mat for the first shedding of dirt on shoes. Your best bet is an outdoor mat without perforations and with a rubber backing. This mat will serve on an exposed stoop or pavement, as well. Consider using a mat large enough to extend beyond the doorjambs by a foot or so, allowing maximum foot-wiping room. Even the door leading into the house from a garage needs a mat. Remember that your car tracks dirt from the road and your driveway, and it makes oily dirt when it drips or when you start the engine.

Once you've installed good mats outside each door, put "Clean exterior mats" on your regular "to do" list. Attention to these few, small surfaces can save you a remarkable amount of indoor work. Make a point, as well, of sweeping porches, garage floors, and door areas weekly. Keeping the doorways clear of dead leaves and grass, grit, and sand means there is less to track inside.

27.

Do Less Better

Many cleaning jobs have the potential to be laborious and time-consuming. They can also be handled intelligently and with a lot less effort. The best cleaning tool that you own is your own good sense. When you put your mind to it, you will see that abiding by a few simple principles allows you to do a better cleaning job with less effort.

Avoid buildup. Whether it's furniture or floor wax, kitchen grease, window grime, drips and small spills in the refrigerator, or grit around the bathroom faucet, it takes half of the time and a quarter of the effort if you stay on top of it. As soon as you ignore it and let it accumulate, you create a cleaning problem that will be heavy on elbow grease and potentially low on results. Catch it while it's fresh, and save the hassle.

Use "the force." Those cleaning solutions that you always keep at hand are designed to make your work easier, but you need to use them properly to get the desired result. That means that you should use as little as you absolutely need. The cleaners themselves can create buildup when they are over-applied. They can also cause damage to certain surfaces. Some cleaning agents when overused can actually break down surfaces. Wood is especially susceptible to damage. Without judicious use of products, any finish can quickly and easily wear away, leaving your wood vulnerable to discoloration and decay.

Do every job right the first time. "A lick-and-a-promise" does not mean that you dust the outer six inches of the bureau top so that you won't have to move the articles on top. All that does is leave half the dust in place while creating a demarcation that makes it all the more obvious that you didn't dust well. At the times that you do a "light" cleaning, dust properly but skip the polish.

In short, work smart. Spot-clean promptly. Use cleaning solutions judiciously. Make whatever amount of effort you invest really count.

28.

Employ Second Glances

In the interest of doing a cleaning job well, keep in mind that it is remarkably easy to overlook something the first time that you deal with it. Get into the habit of "proofreading" your cleaning jobs. Give a room a quick look-see when you've finished it. Make sure you look up, as well as down. Look behind things, as well as on the surfaces. Visually walk through the space, taking into account all of the furnishings that the room holds.

Of course, if you miss something this week, you can catch up with it next week without much loss of your good reputation as a better-than-average housecleaner. However, getting into the habit of proofreading the job when you're done will ensure that your misses are minor and few.

It's a simple, quick bit of thoroughness to take note of the job that you've done. Make it as automatic as the cleaning itself. You'll find that it's so effective a method that you'll want to apply it to other sorts of work and activity.

29.

Create Rewards

One of the reasons that people dislike housecleaning is that it rarely, if ever, delivers a satisfactory sense of closure. No sooner have you brought your home to a spit-and-polish sparkle than dust, lint, dirt, and fingerprints miraculously reappear.

Housecleaning requires definitions all its own. For example, "clean" cannot be construed as a completed outcome, only as a completed action. For a very finite period of time, the objects and surfaces that you clean will be clean. Almost immediately, however, they will start to collect dirt again. You did the work. It's up for grabs how long it will look like that. That's the way it is.

"Finished" is also a relative term when applied to housecleaning. When are you finished with your housework? How can you be finished if the work that you did keeps undoing itself? You see the problem.

Yet it is in the nature of being human that we thrive on a sense of accomplishment. So given the nature of housecleaning, how are we supposed to come out of the job with that happy glow of a job well done?

Try this. Each time that you plan to do some cleaning, make a clearly defined list of the specific jobs that you want to accomplish. Then choose a simple reward for crossing every item off your list. When you've done all of the jobs and crossed them off, consider yourself finished and collect your reward.

For example, suppose you've decided that today you'll do a thorough job on the bathrooms. When that defined work is done, you intend to put your feet up and read that unfinished novel for at least an hour. Maybe your list would look like this.

- Launder bathmats and curtains.
- Disinfect tub and toilet.
- Wash mirrors.
- Polish sink and vanity.
- Dust fixtures and woodwork.
- Spot-clean mildew on ceiling.
- Vacuum.
- Wet-mop floor.

When the list is entirely crossed off, you are finished. Is there more cleaning that could be done? Sure, but that isn't the deal that you made with yourself. It's reading time, and you're in the clear!

30.

Avoid On-Demand Cleaning

Making housecleaning a regular part of your life and schedule has several great virtues. Routine cleaning helps eliminate the big nasty jobs by taking care of them while they're small. It also offers aesthetic and psychological benefits. Most people find a clean, tidy environment pleasing to both the eye and the soul. Many find that other home pursuits—recreation, study, cooking, hobbies—are made more enjoyable when the house is clean and in order.

Perhaps the most rewarding aspect of sticking to the housecleaning schedule is the flexibility that it affords when company comes a-calling. What's worse than a last-minute call from your spouse that she or he is bringing home a colleague—or even the boss? How panicked are you when out-of-town friends "surprise" you with a call from their cell phone informing you that they're pulling into your driveway? What about those family occasions—not surprises, but rarely well-timed in a busy life—when everyone is coming to you for the party? All of these situations, and many others like them, are cause for last-minute, death-defying marathons of cleaning that leave you exhausted and flustered before your guests even arrive.

That is, unless you happen to be in the habit of keeping the housecleaning under control. Any house that gets a good cleaning every week, regular touch-ups in high-traffic areas, consistent spot-cleanings when accidents happen, and a daily de-clutter is ready for company whenever it arrives. The house may not look like you were planning a reception for the president, but it will in no way embarrass you. Your guests will feel comfortable, welcome, and happy to have your relaxed attention, and you'll have the energy to enjoy the people that you love.

31.

Consider Occasional Help

A household in which all of the adults work full-time away from home can run into time constraints that make it difficult to keep up with the full load of housework. This happens, too, in families with preschool children or in-home offices. Just the basic business of keeping everyone fed, in clean clothes, and where they're supposed to be from day to day seems to eat up a huge portion of the available time each week.

If this describes your home, think about your decision to "do it all" yourself. Remember that hiring help never has to be an all-or-nothing proposition. Plenty of professional housecleaners are happy to fill up the holes in their schedules by taking on once- or twice-a-month customers. It's also possible to hire cleaning people for a limited number of hours. Instead of asking them to do the whole house every time, you can assign specific jobs or portions of the whole. From week to week, or on a bimonthly basis, you may change what jobs they do.

Consider, as well, the cleaning services that specifically target big jobs, such as carpet and upholstery cleaning, fall or spring cleaning, draperies, or window washing. These companies send in an expert team with professional equipment, which means that the job can be completed in much less time than it would probably take you to do it. They will give you an estimate before you commit, and their work is generally guaranteed.

You may look to any of these sorts of cleaning services at times of unusual stress or busyness, as well—but look around ahead of time. Get to know who's available in your area. Get some good references, and have a clear sense of how far ahead you need to schedule, as well as what the cost is likely to be. When the stress hits and the last thing that you need is one more problem to solve, you'll already know your options.

Most of the time, our stress level climbs highest when we feel like we're trapped. Don't let housecleaning become your trap. Stay open to creative ways that you can hire help if and when you need it.

32.

Develop Auto-Drive

Any activity that you repeat routinely has the capacity to become automatic. Most people, for example, don't give a lot of thought to brushing their teeth. For health and beauty reasons, they understand that the job must be done a couple of times a day. They don't have to decide when they'll brush because their routine is established. They brush their teeth after breakfast and before bed—while they think, meanwhile, about what would be the perfect gift for Dad's birthday, or how to solve that problem at work. Teeth-brushing happens on auto-drive.

Many aspects of cleaning can be just as straightforward and predictable as brushing your teeth. With relatively little effort, you can establish a routine for the simple, daily cleaning jobs that makes them as effortless and automatic as brushing your teeth. Such activities as making the bed, picking up yesterday's clothes, wiping the kitchen counters, and sweeping the back step can become mindless busywork that you do while you're thinking about the rest of your life.

Bigger jobs also have auto-drive potential. If, for instance, you clean the bathroom every single Saturday morning, right after your shower—a job that can be completed in no more than five or ten minutes if you do some minor daily maintenance—it ceases to be one of the nagging chores hanging over your head. Instead, it's a given that you don't need to even think about. The job gets done automatically.

The key to auto-drive is routine. Repeat the same job at the same time in the same way, day after day, or week after week, and it will become automatic. Take on one or two jobs that tend to nag at you. Find times and methods to complete them that are as efficient as you can make them. Then stick with the routine that you've developed. Repeat it over and over again until it comes naturally. When you've mastered those one or two jobs, move on to the next couple of jobs. Before you know it, half or more of your cleaning will seem like it's doing itself.

33.

Remember the Great Outdoors

Making sure that every entrance to your home has adequate mats and rugs for wiping feet and catching dirt only goes so far. If you want to make your cleaning as low-maintenance as possible, you may want to think about how you handle the terrain beyond your doorstep, as well.

Assess the pathways that people entering your house have to walk. If you have paved walkways and driveway, you have an automatic advantage, because such surfaces don't produce dirt. They can contribute to tracked dirt, however, if you neglect to sweep away sand, grass clippings, mud, or other debris. Get yourself a push broom that is the right width for your walkways, and find a place to store it that makes it easy to pick up and use a few times a week. It doesn't take long to sweep hard, paved surfaces, and your effort is paid back many times over in saved cleaning time.

If you have gravel or stone leading up to your doors, you have a greater challenge. Many shoes are designed with treads that pick up and hold on to stones. Unless you subscribe to the no-shoe policy indoors, those embedded stones can gouge and scratch your floors and create heavy-duty wear and tear on rugs and carpets. Alternatively, the stones may very well dislodge themselves and produce a gritty surface that dirties and damages floors.

You may not want to replace gravel and stone with macadam or concrete, but you can make some compromises that take the crunch out of the paths and driveway. Simply placing larger, flat stepping stones in the gravel along frequently walked paths can eliminate much of the tracked grit. People tend to step from one large stone to the next, sidestepping the small rocks. This can be a great boon to grass or dirt pathways, as well.

Some homeowners have kept the look of gravel or pea stone while creating a more solid surface by using a treatment that compacts the stone or actually binds it. Most home improvement stores have information about such treatments and can advise a do-it-yourselfer on what will work best in his or her situation.

Over years, such changes can pay for themselves in both time and money. Why work harder than you have to? Control the dirt before it ever reaches your door.

34.

Find Pleasure Points

L ife is short, even if you live to a venerable old age. It's a shame not to enjoy every aspect of it that you can. Housecleaning isn't your idea of a high time? That doesn't mean that you have to write it off as one of life's unalleviated miseries. With a little reflection and planning, you can at least find some of the simple pleasures that cleaning affords.

In fact, some people design their housecleaning routines with an eye to eking out every ounce of satisfaction that they can. Do you get a charge out of a spit-and-polish gleam? Make a point of buffing surfaces and hardware in the kitchen and bathroom with a clean, dry towel after you disinfect. That little added touch can give you a lift. Take the time to set out a vase of fresh flowers on a wood surface that you've just polished to a luster. The reflection of the flowers' beauty on the surface of the wood will embellish the work that you've done.

What gives you the biggest charge when you clean? Is it finding the fastest, most efficient way to get through it? Capitalize on that aspect of your temperament. Experiment with different ways of doing the cleaning. Time yourself on particular jobs, and see how you can cut minutes off of each one. Make yourself the household efficiency expert, and glory in the creative solutions that you come up with.

Maybe what you like most is to see big results. In that case, you might derive the greatest pleasure from cleaning by concentrating on one room at a time and doing it from top to bottom—de-clutter to final polish—before you move on to the next room. Perhaps you really appreciate improving the quality of your work. Make it a point to give your attention to that part of what you're doing. Be on the lookout for new ways to smooth the wrinkles out of your cleaning, and then pat yourself on the back every time you put your methods to good use.

Most of all, take the time, even if it's only five minutes of "down-time," to appreciate the results of your work. It's fair, when the cleaning is finished for the day or week, to give yourself a little break in the action to survey what you've accomplished. Let satisfaction and pleasure have their moment before you move on to the next order of your day.

35.
Chart Your Progress

You know the essentials of what you need to do to keep up with your daily and weekly cleaning. You can probably also map out what you'd like to do to stay on target with the bigger, less frequent cleaning jobs. The question is, how do you give yourself the leg up to fulfill your plans?

Consider some simple method of reminders in the form of a chart or list. For the weekly work, it's easy enough to use your desk calendar to just jot in the jobs and when you'll do them. Doing this every week gives you the advantage of looking at the realities of your commitments—not just the regular job- or household-related givens, but also your social engagements, appointments, and other excursions. Actually putting your housecleaning jobs on the calendar helps you know when you're in danger of overloading your life with other items.

Recording your housecleaning on your calendar may also alert you to a week when you have to make do with a lighter cleaning.

Just knowing that you won't have time for a big job can give you the impetus to do a lick-and-a-promise cleaning without guilt or anxiety. Rather than promising yourself the usual thorough cleaning and never getting to it, you can realistically take a moment here and there to do what's absolutely needed.

Tracking your larger cleaning jobs—window washing, carpet cleaning, cleaning the refrigerator and freezer, clearing gutters, and so forth—probably calls for a more generic chart. You can make your own month-by-month checklist for the year in a form that is easy to reproduce, either by photocopy or computer printout. Such a list allows you to fill in items for the month without reference to your current calendar. If you use such a record, you'll see at the beginning of each month what you need to fit in among your other plans. It gives you the opportunity to assign a specific time frame to each job.

Any of these tracking methods allows you not only to plan the work, but also to check it off as you complete it. Cleaning is never really finished, because it keeps undoing itself, but your housecleaning jobs do have a beginning and end. Give yourself credit for what you've accomplished within a given time frame. That list of checked-off items will be a welcome reminder that you're on the job.

36.

Conduct Reviews

Even the most effective routine needs to be revisited from time to time. Your household changes as children grow, hobbies are dropped or added, belongings accumulate, or time commitments swell or shrink. What worked for you last year may now be outdated and ineffective.

Don't despair. Where there's life, there's change. Maintaining any routine, including your housecleaning routine, without reference to such change can become an exercise in frustration. Recognizing the organic nature of life and going with the ebb and flow of it can keep you balanced and productive. That's why it's a good idea to periodically review how your overall cleaning plans are working out.

This is not a big deal. At about the time you find that you are accomplishing less than you used to, or that there are jobs that you just never seem to get to, you know that it's time to look again at what you're doing and how you're doing it. Pinpoint the problem areas—identifiable by the amount of frustration they generate—and consider how you can deal with them more effectively.

Once you've identified your problem areas, give yourself permission to try some new ways of doing the old jobs. Think creatively about whether you need or can afford outside help. Question whether jobs have been adequately delegated among household members. Consider whether there are ways in which you have complicated your housecleaning unnecessarily (as happens, for instance, when you've overloaded a room with furnishings). Ask yourself what would make your tasks more manageable, and look for ways to put your ideas into action.

A little assessing can make a big difference in how well you run your household. Take a breather once in a while simply to think your choices through afresh.

37.

Check Your Stashes

Just as you need to review the way that you do things sometimes, you also need to take stock of what you are accumulating. Belongings can sneak up on you over time. Tools, toys, clothes, and furnishings become obsolete. Saved letters, books, coupons, and recipes lose their appeal or relevance. Medications, foodstuffs, and various supplies pass their expiration dates.

If you aren't in the habit of regularly looking over the items that you store in cabinets, closets, lofts, and the garage, develop the habit now. For starters, commit yourself to going through your refrigerator and pantry to dispose of any outdated foodstuffs and supplies. These items not only take up valuable space, they also constitute a health hazard. Make this a priority.

Second on the list should be your bathroom and linen closet. Dump any medications, whether they are prescription or over-the-counter, that have passed their expiration date. Either use up the dribs and drabs of old supplies, or dispose of them. There's no point in keeping little bits of this and that indefinitely. If you haven't used them, ask yourself why not. It's probably because you've found other products that you prefer.

Once you've started such sorting with an eye to paring down your belongings, you may find it addictive. While the impulse is strong, pick a storage place and go at it. If you're dealing with a large space, commit yourself only to what you can accomplish in the amount of time that you have available right now. For example, if you have a couple of hours on a summer afternoon, make up your mind to pull the boxes out of the north corner of the attic. Just that one corner. Do the job completely, keeping only what you really want or will need and storing it in well-marked containers that can be neatly stowed. The next time that you have a bit more time, move on to the next chunk of storage in the attic. If you have a disaster in your closet, commit yourself to one job at a time. "Today, I go through belts and shoes. Next week, I pull out all the clothes I haven't worn for a year."

Give yourself the gift of clearing out the stashes in your house. Over time, they can come to weigh on you in ways that you may not even realize. As you bring them to order and remove the excess, you'll gain a growing sense of satisfaction and clarity.

38.

Share the Wealth

One of the best results of cleaning out your storage areas is the opportunity to share your abundance with others. A bounty of organizations exist to make your excess belongings available to others who may have a need or desire for them.

Consider donating goods to clothing banks. These charitable organizations sort through used clothes and distribute them to people who lack the means to buy what they need. Your out-of-date coat may be the difference between warmth and chill to someone in need. Your slightly worn athletic shoes may allow someone to replace shoes with no soles.

Think, as well, about donating toys, games, and books to community centers, hospitals, or public libraries. Assuming that your castoffs meet safety standards, you may be able to help equip a daycare center or a hospital playroom. The equipment in many of these busy facilities sees enough wear and tear that they need to replace what they have regularly. Most public libraries have yearly book sales that benefit the library and allow them to update their own collections and meet operating expenses.

You may also discover that you have unused treasures lurking in your overstocked house. Goodwill and the Salvation Army are always happy to accept furnishings in good repair. In turn, they give away or sell at a discount those items to people who could not otherwise afford furnishings or who appreciate used goods. Consignment shops will take your items and sell them for you, adding some percentage to your asking price as a commission. The net result for you is some income and freed-up storage space.

The material abundance of modern life is both a blessing and curse for most of us. You can tip the balance toward the positive by letting your wealth spill over onto others less fortunate.

39.

Use Downtime

It's a hallmark of modern life that we never seem to have enough time for all that we need or want to do. Jobs, activities, social engagements, and routine appointments keep us running. From the time that we rise in the morning until we hit the sack at night, we have one eye on the clock and the other on the calendar. The very idea of carving hours out of an overloaded schedule for housecleaning every week feels like a bad joke.

Yet look more closely, and you may discover that there's more time available in your day for cleaning than you think. It takes the form of dozing in front of the television, surfing the Internet, playing computer games, leafing through junk mail, and window shopping at the local mall. It may seem to you that there's therapeutic value in such pastimes, and certainly there can be. However, the relaxation value goes out the window if such activities eat up discretionary time while your nerves fray over all that you never seem to get done.

Keep track of your time over one typical week. Write down everything that you do—including the twenty-minute nap, or the computer solitaire game—and how long it takes. Be completely thorough and honest. At the end of the week, add up the time that your typical activities take, and you'll begin to see the ways in which your minutes and hours leak out of your day.

Now consider what would happen if you chose to use only some of that time to take care of small housecleaning jobs. What if you dusted a couple of rooms in lieu of watching a half-hour sitcom (which is a rerun anyway)? How about if you chose not to play solitaire so that you could quickly wipe fingerprints off the doorjambs and light switches? What if you took ten extra minutes at makeup time to wipe down the bathroom sink and counters?

The point is that the time to stay on top of housecleaning jobs exists in your days. If you think more in terms of small pieces of the work, and pay attention to ways in which you presently waste the small amounts of time that those jobs take, you can begin to build simple habits that make the housework easier. You don't have to dispense with all of your downtime. Just redeem some small part of it each day. As you do, you'll gain the relaxation value of being on top of what needs to be done.

40.

Use Phone Time

Never before has the telephone played such an omnipresent role in people's lives. With the advent of cordless home phones and cell phones, people can go anywhere and do anything without forgoing or disconnecting a call. This has its benefits in increased ease of contact with loved ones and business associates, but it has some obvious drawbacks, as well. We forget about the safety problems associated with driving a car while talking on a phone and the courtesy issues of using cell phones in restaurants, theaters, and other public venues. It's enough to simply recognize that with almost limitless access, telephones can and often do take over hours of our lives.

So what does this have to do with housecleaning? Because cordless phones with the gear to make them hands-free can travel all over the house with you, you have the potential to make a lot of conversation time serve more than one purpose. Phone time offers the perfect opportunity for you to work your way through the house, doing a wide variety of cleaning jobs that require no concentration and make no noise.

One great use of phone time is de-cluttering. When you get on the phone, choose any room in the house, and start picking up the out-of-place items. If they have a home in that room, put them away. If they belong somewhere else, choose a spot to accumulate items that need to go elsewhere. As soon as the room is straightened, grab the items that you've accumulated and carry them to their rightful places. Then choose another room and repeat the process. Depending on how long you tend to talk, you can tidy up an entire house while you catch up with a good friend.

Think about some of the quiet jobs that you don't take the time to do on a typical cleaning day—washing or dusting the leaves of a houseplant, wiping down window blinds, dusting the lamps, fixtures, or books on the shelf. Such jobs don't need to be done every week—just from time to time. For that reason, it's easy to forget them or put them off. However, they can take some of the sting out of being put on hold by the doctor's office or a mail-order service department. While you wait, you can do something of value and lighten your cleaning load.

The telephone, in whatever form it takes next, will probably be with us for some time to come. Make the most of its convenience and portability by checking a few cleaning jobs off your list while you talk.

41.

Use Dream Time

The more routine your housecleaning becomes, the easier you'll find it to make the most of that time. So much of the work that you do around the house requires little or no concentration. You repeat the actions so often that they virtually do themselves. You can choose to see such work as tedious and boring, or you can see it as the perfect time to dream.

Dream time is when you think about plans for the future. It's when you figure out the perfect birthday gift for someone special. It's also the time when you think through how to handle a thorny problem, concoct a great party idea, or plan your spring garden. In other words, it's your "bright idea" time.

Everybody dreams, especially when their activities are relatively "mindless." You can carve dream time out of your housecleaning time most effectively by planning it into your routine. To begin with, tuck a pen and piece of paper or small notebook in your pocket before you start cleaning. Then, as you start to clean, consciously focus your attention on some particular subject that is calling for mental attention. As you think and dream about the subject, capture good ideas—your personal brainstorming—on the paper that you're carrying. This will help ensure that you later remember some of the solutions or ideas that you came up with.

Keep in mind that dream time can just as easily turn into brooding time. Perhaps you've had a fight with your spouse or you just found out that you're short of money for the month. Resist the temptation to let your thoughts spiral into negativity. Instead, reserve your housecleaning dreaming for productive, creative thought. Make it such a habit that the minute you pick up a dust cloth or pull out the vacuum, your wheels automatically start turning on positive solutions and bright new ideas. It may not actually teach you to love the time that you spend cleaning, but it will certainly make the most of your time—and it may just brighten your day.

42.

Clean As You Go

Your house never needs to fall into total disarray. A clean-as-you-go style of life can keep everything in relatively good order between serious cleaning times. The net results are a more pleasant day-to-day environment and a much lighter load when cleaning day comes around.

For example, every time that you get ready to use the kitchen for food preparation, make it a habit to begin by filling a dishpan with hot soapy water. As you finish with a utensil or bowl, put it straight into the dishpan. As soon as you have a free moment—while something sautés, bakes, or rises—do a mini washup. In less than your total cooking time, you'll be close to finished with the cleaning up. All that will be left is loading the dishwasher with dishes that you use for serving the meal.

The bathroom is another likely spot for cleaning as you go. It only takes five minutes after a shower, for instance, to squeegee and wipe down the tiles and fixtures. When you're through with the sink, a quick squirt with window cleaner and a paper towel buffing will leave the basin and vanity looking freshly scoured. In both cases, you avoid soap and hard water buildup—thus cutting down on the amount of cleansers and chemicals that you introduce into the environment—while leaving the bathroom ready for a surprise, drop-in guest.

You can keep the clutter down by providing hooks for easy hanging of such items as jackets, exercise clothes, robes, and pajamas. Placing small trash baskets in every room will make it as simple to dispose of trash promptly as to leave it where it was made.

Get in the habit of wiping up small spills right away. Quickly take a dustpan and brush to the grit that you notice by a door or on the kitchen floor. When you change clothes, put the ones that you're taking off directly into the hamper or on a hanger instead of dropping them on the floor or over the back of a chair.

None of these jobs takes more than a few minutes by themselves. Let them accumulate, though, and you've got a mess to clean up. Why not clean as you go and lighten your load?

43.

Think Ahead

There are times when you really want your house to shine. Special occasions, infrequent guests, or a particularly important visitor may make the business of housecleaning unusually stressful for you. Happily, such times rarely crop up at the last minute. You have plenty of lead time to think ahead about just how clean you want your home to be—and how to make it that way.

Make the most of advance warning. In the same way that you give careful thought to the food that you'll serve and the clothes that you'll wear, take the time to look around the house and see what needs to be done. Make a list of every housecleaning job that you'd like to accomplish before your guest or event arrives. If there are particular items that are not part of the weekly cleaning routine—silver to polish, lamps to clean, flowers to arrange—make sure to include these on the list.

Once you know what needs to happen, look realistically at the amount of time that you have before the event. Some jobs can be done well in advance. Others are, by their nature, last-minute items. Pace yourself by planning to spread the jobs out, tackling one or two day by day. In other words, put a time frame on your to-do list.

If you find that there's more to do than time to do it, you have two choices. One, you can go over your list and cross out the items that are more "wish list" than "must-do." Alternatively, you can figure out how to divide the labor among more people, either by delegating jobs to family or household members or by hiring out some part of the work. In either case, you'll avoid the trap of discovering only at the last moment that you can't do it all.

There's nothing wrong with a little adrenaline in your bloodstream for an important occasion, but when you cross over into panic, it can rob you of the pleasure and satisfaction that such an occasion has the potential to give you. Think of yourself as "home manager," and plan ahead for the big deals in your life. Don't let the cleaning jobs undo you. Pace yourself and space them out so that you can have as good a time as you give your guests.

44.

Suit Your Style

Nothing causes more daily stress than to live out of sync with who you are and what you really care about. You have a unique blend of temperament, personality, circumstances, and values. Your aspirations and concerns play into your choices and habits in unique ways. No one can tell you, ultimately, what is best for you or what will give you the greatest satisfaction and meaning. Only you know.

Housecleaning may not seem like one of the big things to consider, in terms of overall quality of life. A lot of people view it as nothing more than a necessary evil to be gotten through as quickly as possible. Yet it plays such a consistent role in the average life, and takes such a significant amount of effort, that perhaps we would be better served to give it its due as a real factor in our happiness and well-being. In that case, housecleaning—just as surely as occupation, location, or other lifestyle choices—needs to be handled in a way that "fits" who we are or want to be.

Do you aspire to a relaxed, user-friendly way of life? Then let your housecleaning reflect that. Loosen the reins on how impeccable your place needs to be before a guest can cross the threshold. Spend less attention on the details of spotlessness and more on the elements of comfort. Alternately, do you thrive on creating beauty and elegance around you? Then suit your cleaning routines to the demands of a showplace, knowing that the effort will yield rewards for your soul, as well as your eyes.

While some people may lose sleep over trying to keep up appearances that matter more to others than to themselves, others will hyperventilate over what they personally perceive as a slovenly environment. You fall somewhere on the scale. Know yourself and what you care about. Then suit your housecleaning to your style.

45.

Choose Your Friends

Most of us care what others think of us. We want to be liked and respected. We want to fit in. However, sometimes the people in our lives are not particularly similar to us. While there's much to be said for the interest and stimulation that friends offer when they are different from us, there's also sometimes a price to pay as we try to win approval and acceptance from people with dissimilar values. The wider the gap between the expectations of others and our natural inclinations, the more difficult we find it to be comfortable and at peace with them or ourselves.

One of the arenas in which we feel this most acutely is in our homes. We want to be able to entertain friends. We want to open our doors. Yet what we observe of our friends' homes and the ways that they keep those homes can leave us insecure and feeling inadequate.

Don't fall into the trap of surrounding yourself with people whose values and lifestyles create burdensome pressure on the way you live. "Keeping up with the Joneses" doesn't apply solely to material possessions. It can just as surely rule the way that you keep your house. If you're living according to someone else's views, you can be sure that the business of housecleaning will be far more onerous than it needs to be.

Distinguish friends from acquaintances, people who happen to live in your neighborhood, and extended family. You will undoubtedly have plenty of give and take with the latter two categories of people, but you can learn to keep a level head about their opinions of you and how you do things. You can adopt a live-and-let-live attitude, which means that you decide neither to judge them nor to take their judgments to heart.

Friends are a different matter. We invest ourselves in our friends. We care about their opinions, and they care about ours. In the best of circumstances, we and our friends take part in one another's growth and development over time. That's why it's important to choose friends wisely. Good friends bring out the best in you. They appreciate you for who you are and support you in being true to yourself.

If you have friends who routinely raise the stress level in your life—if friends judge you for the way that you keep your house or the cleaning style that you're comfortable with—reconsider the quality of those friendships. You can choose friends who understand and like the person that you are.

46.

Simplify Entertaining

Sometimes, we set ourselves up for more housekeeping than is necessary. This is especially true when it's time to roll out the red carpet for guests. In the interest of impressing people or making them feel important, we plan meals, events, or hospitality that test our endurance and squeeze our precious time.

The next time that you make plans to entertain, think carefully about every aspect of your intentions. In the marketing world, experts often apply a "theory of diminishing returns" to their advertising strategies. They understand, by studying past sales results, that an ad campaign can actually be too expensive and elaborate to be worth the relatively minimal gain in buyers. The same basic principle can be applied in real estate. Certain improvements may help you sell your property at an appreciable gain, but too many can mean that you cannot even recover your expenses in a resale.

The theory of diminishing returns can be just as valid when you entertain. If the housecleaning associated with entertaining puts you over the edge, think about what you're doing and why. Consider whether anyone other than you would really notice the difference if you did just a little less decorating or made a simpler meal. Sort out which of your cleaning and associated activities are important enough to consider "must-do" items. You may discover that you've assigned the same priority to all of the possible setup jobs, when in fact some of them could be neglected with little or no harm to the enjoyment of your guests.

If you happen to be the kind of person who gets a thrill out of doing things in a big way for guests and parties, then go for it. Just keep in mind that there really is only so much time in the day and so much energy in your veins. If you want to put a load of effort into the event and deal with all of the cleaning that it involves before and after, figure out what other parts of your life will get some leeway. Your guests will have a far better time if you're relaxed and happy than if you're exhausted or tense. Make your entertainment only as involved as it has to be to give you and your guests the good time that you hope for.

47.

Put First Things First

Oone of the keys to good time management is prioritizing. Some things actually matter more than others. They produce more negative effects when you neglect them. It makes sense, then, to put these things at the top of your list when you're figuring out how, when, and what to do from day-to-day in relation to housecleaning.

Keep a running priority list in your mind as you deal with your housecleaning. The list will probably change from day to day. Some jobs—such as washing windows or waxing floors—can be put off for a while, but they eventually become critical. That means that over time, they work their way up the priority list. Other jobs—such as sanitizing bathrooms or kitchens—never lose their high rank for long. If you learn to think in terms of priority, you'll find it far easier to decide what jobs can be postponed if necessary. You'll also avoid living with unneeded stress over things that you should have done but failed to accomplish.

If you don't have a ready sense of what really matters in housecleaning and what doesn't, it is probably simply because you haven't taken sufficient time to think it through. Remember that the whole issue of priorities tends to be a personal one. If you share your household with a partner or spouse, your priorities will need to take that person's ideas into account. Ultimately, however, your priorities will be dictated by what you care most about.

Following your priority list—putting first things first—can help you experience the full potential of satisfaction from your cleaning efforts. It's so easy to fritter away your time doing a little of this and a little of that. When you come up short on time for the jobs that you consider important, you feel ineffectual and frustrated. If, instead, you focus from the start on at least finishing the most critical jobs, you'll waste a lot less time on the minor chores and earn a sense of accomplishment that rewards your efforts.

48.

Consider the Source

For many people, the response of others to their housecleaning efforts is a major factor in negative feelings about the work. This is completely understandable, especially since the one in a household who does the lion's share of the work often does it at least as much for the benefit of others as for him- or herself. Unfortunately, it's a fact of life that praise and appreciation are more often in short supply than not.

Instead of suffering over negative feedback or lack of acknowledgment, put these responses in perspective. Consider the source. For example, if your family members show a notable lack of appreciation for all that is involved in housecleaning, keep in mind that most or all of them have never had the housecleaning buck stop with them. They honestly have no idea what it feels like to know that if you don't do it, it won't get done. For the most part, they've probably never been responsible for more than a few designated jobs—which, by the way, they didn't even have to discover or keep track of for themselves.

In the case of your children, you'll probably have to wait until they have homes of their own or share dorm space with other young people before they begin to appreciate all that you provided for them. If your spouse is a problem, you probably need to communicate more clearly how important some appreciation is to you. You may also have to share the workload more meaningfully so that he or she has a more realistic view of all that you do.

Parents often criticize the lifestyle and decisions of their adult children. If your parents have negative things to say about how you keep your house, try to remember that for some years, they actually bore the responsibility of teaching you how to do such things as clean the house. In-laws, too, tend to have opinions about what you do and how you do it. In their case, negative responses often arise out of the sense that they've "lost" their child (or sibling) to you and your influence. Exercise some compassion and generosity. Let them know, in one way or another, that their importance has not diminished. It has simply changed. Communicate, as well, that you respect their ideas, even if you don't entirely agree with them.

People are the way that they are for reasons. When other people make it hard for you to have a positive attitude about housecleaning, try to put yourself in their shoes and figure out why they don't support you. You may discover that what they need is a little appreciation from you.

49.

Be Your Own Best Friend

What makes the opinions of others so important to us? Often, we look to others to affirm and approve of us because we have doubts about ourselves. Believe it or not, this tendency exhibits itself in even as mundane a matter as how we keep house. We don't fret and fuss over how the house looks in a vacuum (forgive the pun). We judge ourselves harshly for our relative lack of skill or timeliness in keeping a clean house insofar as we think others do.

Maybe you have wonderful friends and family members around you who notice and cheer. If so, you have something to be thankful for. Whether you receive a lot of support or not, however, you can be your own best friend. Give yourself some credit for all that you do and what it takes to do it. Remember to offer yourself some pats on the back for the efforts that you invest in your home. You're the only one who knows your situation intimately. That means that only you can truly understand what you do and why.

There's more to friendship than good times, though. A good friend also accepts your shortfalls. Be your own best friend when you do less than you'd like around the house. Forgive yourself when you wear out before the job is done. Let it go when you have other, unexpected demands that eat up your time, you come down with the flu, succumb to cabin fever, or accept an invitation too good to refuse. You don't have to achieve perfection in your housecleaning to be happy with yourself. You can even fail to do it altogether and be okay.

Some people have an easier time than others dealing with the frailties of being human. In reality, though, we all have our ups and downs, our successes and failures. No one thrives under the criticism of an unforgiving eye, and that includes the criticism that comes from yourself. Be a friend to you.

50.

Rearrange the Furniture

In the business of housecleaning, little inefficiencies can add a load to your work that is both frustrating and unnecessary. Take a look around the spaces you clean. How easily can you move your cleaning equipment around your furnishings? Do the floor nozzles of your vacuum cleaner fail to fit handily between pieces of furniture? Do you have inconvenient nooks and crannies created by the decorative items that you've chosen? Have you crammed an excess of items into any room to the point that you dread the moment that you have to clean it?

You don't have to suffer the inconveniences that you've created. Many different considerations go into the way that anyone furnishes or decorates his or her home. There's every reason to make one of those considerations cleaning efficiency. When you're in the market for new furnishings, take size and shape into account. A little breathing room between pieces of furniture and other decorative items makes cleaning a great deal easier. Think about what it will take to reach corners, baseboards, carpet edges, and bare floors, depending on what you place in a room and where you put it. It takes only a small effort to plan for cleaning. It creates hours of labor if you ignore it.

If you've already made your furnishing decisions, assess where you are. If you regularly deal with hard-to-reach spaces that require a gymnast's skill to overcome, you may want to think about rearranging the furniture. A subtle shift of position can sometimes open the space needed for a mop or floor attachment. Creating rooms within rooms by arranging furniture in conversation groupings can give you clearer access to baseboards and carpet edges. Opening space for easy traffic through a room can also make for freer movement while cleaning.

Remember, too, that you may just have more furnishings than you need. If your home is too crowded for comfort or efficiency, experiment with eliminating something. Put it in storage for a couple of weeks, get used to the way that the room looks without it, and see how you do. You may find that simpler is better in more ways than one.

51.

Redecorate

Reducing your home maintenance may call for an overhaul in your thinking. Obviously, different folks find different styles pleasing—but if cleaning your home has become your nemesis in part because you've chosen a style of decorating that creates work, it wouldn't hurt to look into a different style.

Think, for example, about whether you could achieve as pleasing an effect by concentrating collectibles in several showcase areas rather than spreading them throughout a room or house. A seashell lover does not need to have shells on every available surface. By placing a collection of shells on a tray that can be moved at cleaning time or by choosing only a few shells to display in one place at a time, the shell lover eliminates unwelcome cleaning complications. The same can be said for nearly any collectible. Many people have further reduced their cleaning load by putting collectibles behind glass. This keeps the dust to a minimum and has the added value of protecting the items from damage.

If your decorating style tends to be busy, you may consider mixing the busier elements of your decorating with accents of simplicity. Sometimes, less really is more in creating an atmosphere. Furnishings with lots of nooks and crannies that collect dust and grime can be combined successfully with some that have simpler lines.

You may find that it pays, in terms of cleaning, to use slipcovers that can be laundered rather than relying strictly on costly upholstery that requires special cleaning. Be aware, too, that the colors you choose for furniture, floors, and carpets make a difference in how much dirt and lint show, which can affect how often you feel that you have to clean.

You may not want cleaning considerations to rule your every decorating decision. Just keep in mind that your choices do dictate how high- or low-maintenance your home becomes.

52.

Think Double-Duty

Any way that you can make cleaning easier or more efficient will decrease the stress associated with it. That means that if you can accomplish two things at once, you'll save not only time but trouble.

Whenever you find that you need to do a small cleaning job, consider expanding it just a little to make the interruption worth as much as possible. Is there junk on the bathroom mirror that you can't stand to see for one more morning? When you pull out the window cleaner and paper towel, take an extra moment to hit the surfaces of the vanity and toilet, too. Did someone deposit a shoe-load of mud as they crossed the carpet? Vacuum the whole rug, the whole room, or the whole story of your house while you have the machine out and running. Often, it's the inconvenience of pulling out supplies or a tool that makes people put off their cleaning jobs. Anytime that you absolutely have to use such items, you might as well make the most of them.

When you're looking for an unusual decorating touch for your house, consider making it something that can serve as a cleaning aid. Baskets, for example, add a warm, textural touch to many rooms. They can also serve to contain or conceal newspapers and magazines that you still want to read, small items that you want to have on hand, or mail and papers waiting for attention. One clever reproduction of an earlier basket style is designed to sit on a stair. This can be a tidy repository for items waiting to be taken up- or downstairs in a multilevel house.

Some cleaning tools are actually designed to be displayed. If you have a fireplace or wood stove—notable sources of dirt in the form of ash and wood—an attractive broom-and-pan set that's nice enough to hang in view can make it much easier to clean up the mess as you go. In bygone times, only the upper crust invested in decorations that had no useful purpose. We would do well to learn from the simpler folk how to better join form and function when we decorate.

Watch for opportunities to streamline your cleaning. Think double-duty whenever you can. Double-duty often means half the time.

53.

Love Your Plants

The true plant lover will probably relish the cleaning chores that are necessary to keep plants in good form. It can give you a delightful break to sit at the kitchen table with a cup of tea and a broad-leafed plant, while you gently wash the leaves with a mild soap solution. You can pass a pleasant half hour moving from plant to plant with flower shears and a trash bag, patiently trimming off wilted leaves and blossoms, clipping leggy growth, and removing deadwood. The regular rounds of water and food can feel like a walk around the neighborhood, visiting with good friends. Far from increasing unwanted work, plants for such people offer the pleasure and satisfaction of involvement with living creatures.

Are you such a plant lover? If not, and you keep living plants in your home, count the cost. The care described above is the minimum that you need to do, so choose plants that have a reputation as pest-resistant. Concentrate your efforts on plants that are happiest left alone rather than fussed over. You'll probably want to avoid flowering plants, which only look presentable if you stay on top of pruning and deadheading. Obtain at least a rudimentary education on the simple tricks for avoiding houseplant pests. Any garden center offers literature on the subject, and the public library is teeming with books that will be of help.

If you want the visual advantage of plants in the house without all of the bother, take a look at the latest in silk plants. Unlike their plastic predecessors, the best of these artificial beauties look real enough to fool you, no matter how close you get. They lack the environmental benefits of living plants, but they also lack the living problems. They'll still collect dust, of course, but cleaning is a cinch if you give them a once-a-month vacuuming with the dust nozzle and low suction.

Know yourself in relation to plants. Living flora involve responsibility that delights some and discourages others. If you adore the business of plant maintenance, go for it. Otherwise, choose realistically and avoid the burden of unwanted work.

54.

Lose Your Dust Bunnies

Dust bunnies live in corners, under beds, behind sofas, and between furnishings that are placed too close for convenience. They collect without effort, out of sight, and—if you're in the habit of cleaning only what you see—undetected. Many people either forget them or ignore them, figuring that what you don't see won't hurt (or embarrass) you. If you want the cleaning that you do to last a while, however, this is far from true.

Keep in mind a couple of truths about the dust bunnies. First of all, they are by nature quite lightweight. That means that if they've collected on any hard surface, it takes only the slightest passing whiff of a breeze to move them. They can easily get blown into the open, which is why you may spend a morning cleaning and come back to a dusty floor in the afternoon.

Second, dust bunnies grow over time. They're not called "bunnies" for nothing. Left to their own devices, they multiply. In a very short time, one or two little dust tumblers can became a solid coating of dust that sends more dirt into the atmosphere of your home and becomes more of a challenge to clean when you finally get to it. What's more, it readily mixes with any grease or oil in the air—from cooking or your heating system—to create truly obnoxious grime that you have to scrub to remove.

It only takes a bit of consciousness and an extra moment or two to hit the dust bunny nests in your house. Remember to run the vacuum or mop under furniture, as well as around it. Carry a crevice tool or dusting wand to reach into the narrow spaces that collect the little critters. Work your cleaning tools all the way into corners, even if those corners are not visible to the casual eye. Such simple measures will keep both the dust bunny population and your frustration level to a minimum.

55.

Create Still Lifes

There's no question that clutter creates work when it's time to clean. Ten small objects on the surface of a coffee table or shelf make dusting a lot more work than a clear surface. Yet many of us enjoy the visual effect of decorative touches and relish the sight of mementos and framed family photographs.

You don't have to put away your favorite objects in order to cut down on cleaning woes. You can simplify by taking those items and consolidating them into arrangements that are more easily moved and cleaned. For example, placing a collection of small items on an appropriate tray or holder can allow you to move everything at once when it's time to clean the furniture that they sit on. The items themselves may not have to be cleaned as often as the tabletop or other surface, and you can get the job done quickly and without fudging.

It can help, as well, to place items in such a way that you can easily wipe around them for the lick-and-a-promise cleanings that can suffice in a pinch. Rather than loading as many separate decorative pieces as possible onto a single surface, pare down what you display. Restrain the impulse to add. Instead, step back and really look at what you're doing. Be selective, and work for an artistic touch that is simple and elegant. You don't have to put everything that you have on show. You can trade off what you display from time to time. Not only will you lessen your cleaning work, you'll show off what you have to better effect and introduce some variety into your decorating from time to time.

Beautifying a home can be heartwarming and rewarding. It pays, though, to keep in mind what impact your decorating will have on cleaning day. A thoughtful approach will save cleaning steps and time.

56.

Escape Paper

Most people find themselves inundated not only with conventional mail but with a broad variety of catalogs, advertising sheets, free newspapers, junk mail, and periodicals. Some of this comes to you because you've requested it. A lot comes whether you want it or not. The result is a load of paper clutter that gathers on kitchen counters, coffee tables, and desks.

You can get the paper flow under control with a couple of simple habits. The essential trick is to move the paper out just as quickly as it comes in. There's nothing more discouraging (or unsightly) as a growing pile of unread mail and papers. Don't let the pile grow. In fact, don't create the pile in the first place.

Start with what arrives in your mailbox. You probably pick up your mail daily. You can just as readily stand next to a wastebasket and make a quick pass through the stuff before you ever set it on a surface in your house.

Any self-evident junk mail can be tossed immediately in the can. All bills ought to be reviewed right away for accuracy and then placed in the designated spot for storing unpaid bills—an in-basket, desk drawer, or whatever; not an uncontained pile. If you're lucky enough to still receive snail-mail letters, ditto for them.

As for the periodicals and purchased newspapers, take a realistic view of your time. Keep only the most recent issue or two of any publication, and cycle the prior issues into the recycling bin. If you receive a daily newspaper, think daily. The news has changed by the time that you read the daily paper. You don't need to save it once the day is done. If there's some particular article or ad that you want to hold on to, take a moment right away to clip it out, and recycle the rest of the paper.

Ask at your local post office, as well, whether any means exist to avoid receiving unwanted publications and ads. In some cases, you may be able to actually reduce what you receive in the first place.

Most important, don't procrastinate where paper is concerned. Most communities today provide you with easy means to recycle almost every kind of paper that you use or receive. Take advantage of that to keep down the clutter at home while you do your part for the environment.

57.

Find Outlets

An important part of housecleaning involves eliminating material to keep your storage and your cleaning under control. Recycling is one way of eliminating your clutter. You can also find outlets for various items that you no longer want or need.

Talk to your local library about magazines and especially books that are taking up space in your home. Check with local churches and daycare centers when you're struggling with the overflow of neglected toys and children's furnishings. The items that your children have outgrown may be just what a low-budget organization is looking for.

Often, school groups or scout troops have drives for items that can be recycled. Community and church groups sometimes run annual tag sales to benefit their organizations and will welcome contributions that you would consider "white elephants."

You might be storing old tools, pots and pans, utensils, or furnishings that someone could use. Why not give or sell those items instead of taking up valuable space with them?

58.

Create a Filing System

A filing system? Doesn't everyone have one? Believe it or not, something as simple as a central filing system for home records and important papers does not make it onto everyone's radar screen. As a result, much time—and sometimes money—is lost because of materials that have been misplaced or accidentally thrown away. Alternatively, the materials are at hand, but they're disorganized.

Everyone should at least provide their household with a fireproof, file-size box in which to keep vital papers, such as insurance policies, birth records, wills, passports, marriage licenses, and so forth. The loss of such documents causes endless hassle and inconvenience, and in fact can be a source of stolen identity. Not only do you want to use a container that resists fire, you want to be able to lock it.

It helps to have a good system and organized space for materials of lesser value, as well. Establishing one place for all the warrantees, guarantees, owner's manuals, and information sheets on household appliances and tools takes the mystery out of the solution when one of these items breaks down or needs a replacement part. Even a shoebox on a shelf in a utility closet will serve. Better yet, if you own a filing cabinet and have room in it, you can dedicate a drawer or part of a drawer to such documents.

Clearly, you need a designated place, too, for documents relating to your financial matters, including tax returns and the records required by the government. Keeping these materials in good order makes the preparation of home budgets and tax returns far easier than if you routinely scatter your papers throughout the house in various drawers and bins. In the unwanted event that you are audited, you'll make your life a lot easier if you've consistently kept good records and filed them in one system.

A good filing system comes in handy for a variety of other materials, as well, whether they are keepsakes, notes on pleasure trips, your children's or your own school records, family recipes, or ideas clipped from magazines for renovating your house. Whatever the record that you want to keep for later reference, put it in the system. You'll eliminate mess, protect the papers that you save, and make them readily accessible when you need them.

59.

Sort by Sort

The better organized that you are, the less time you'll spend scratching your head over where to put something away or where to find it when you need it. When you're tidying up, think in terms of categories. How you define a category is entirely up to you.

What is the appropriate organizing theme, for example, when the spice shelf needs straightening up? Instead of a higgledy-piggledy pile of bottles and boxes, you might choose to arrange the spices so that finding them and putting them away is quick and efficient. Maybe you'll go for the alphabetical approach. Perhaps you'll want to arrange them according to how often you use them.

The same can be said for clothes, tools, linens, pantry items, or cleaning supplies. You can sort by season, type of item, typical combinations, or even colors. You may have to stand some ribbing if you organize well, but don't let it bother you for a minute. Chances are that the teasers are just jealous. You've managed to make your life easier by creating some order in your house.

60.

Sort by Location

Once everything in your house has a place to be when it's not in use, keeping the clutter down becomes easy. When you pick up, mentally or physically sort misplaced items according to their proper location. Create a standard place where you always put items that need to go back upstairs or downstairs. Make a pile or stack of items for a specific room or storage area, and transport all of the items to a particular location at one time so that you save time and steps.

You may also want to share the job of tidying by making stacks or piles of items that belong to other members of your household. If you have a utility room or hallway that could accommodate it, you may want to designate a central "pickup area" for family members' clutter. Leave it to them to retrieve their belongings and put them where they belong.

If you're raising children, you can reinforce the lesson of their responsibility for their own things by putting a time limit on how long items can go unclaimed. If you designate three days for picking up belongings, at the end of that time period, pack the unclaimed items away in a box. Make the kids work for the return of their things, either by improving their performance over a period of time or by volunteering for some extra jobs around the house. Set a time limit on earning things back, as well. You can be sure that there will only be one or two instances when they find out you gave that special jacket to the clothing bank or that favorite toy to a local charity before they begin to value and care for their belongings in a more appropriate way. Just be sure that everyone understands the rules ahead of time.

Experiment a bit with ways to organize and return your clutter to its proper place. Once you find logic for the job that makes sense to you, you'll find that the job becomes easier—maybe even automatic.

61.

Store in Containers

The huge market in all manner of bins, baskets, boxes, and tubs makes it easier than ever for a household to put things away neatly and store them compactly. The containers fit nearly any budget and are carried in a wide variety of retail outlets, including department stores, supermarkets, discount home goods stores, drugstores, hardware stores, and catalogs. They come in all shapes, sizes, and materials, designed for specific uses or made for general use of any kind. They range from the most utilitarian, plastic models to rather pricey, furniture-quality items that make a good appearance even in public places.

Any item that is small enough to be stored in multiples is a good candidate for containers. Sorting and labeling materials in containers means that you can readily see what you have where. Less rummaging as you try to locate something leads to less mess in the process.

Containers make it possible to store items that otherwise become clutter. A drawer full of desk items soon becomes a "junk" drawer.

Divide the various items into drawer-deep bins, and you have yourself an easily accessed store of desk supplies that stay neat and separate.

A container full of children's craft supplies can become the magic box that you pull out on a rainy afternoon. The real magic, though, takes place when it's time to put all those pens, pencils, scissors, crayons, paper, glitter, and glue away. Everything goes back into the box—or even into smaller containers that then go into the box—and with one quick motion, you can put the whole kit away.

Once you start organizing and storing with containers, you'll probably discover an amazing number of ways that you can solve past storage mess problems. You'll also find that what you store remains cleaner and fresher while it's in storage, which will eliminate extra work when you're ready to use the various items.

62.

Live Within Your Space

Generally speaking, buying habits in the Western world far exceed material needs, with the result that people keep outgrowing their homes, create trash that their towns can't accommodate, and burden themselves with more than they can properly care for or store. A bigger house means expanded acreage to furnish and clean. Excess trash means environmental woes for everyone. Additionally, excess material possessions become clutter, waste, cramped quarters, and unwieldy amounts of items in storage.

If any of this rings true for you, maybe it's time to rethink the modern mantra of "shop 'til you drop." You may find it next to impossible to escape the constant message of materialism, but you can choose how you respond. There's no question, the more that you accumulate, the heavier the load that you carry. That includes your housecleaning.

Try putting a few commonsense ideas to work for you. First, never buy on impulse. Retailers and advertisers work hard to lure you into the impulse buy, because that's the most likely way to get you to spend on items that you wouldn't otherwise want. If you didn't know you needed something until you saw it in the store, chances are that you really don't need it. If you go away and think about it for a few days, and it still seems right to buy the item, later is soon enough.

Second, carefully consider your purchases with an eye to where you'll put them when you take them home. If you find yourself scratching your head, you probably don't have room for the items without ridding yourself of something that you already own. That's certainly an option. On the other hand, do you need to replace what you have? Will the thrill of the purchase last long enough to be worth the price?

People who have chosen to simplify their homes, belongings, and lifestyle almost universally extol the virtues of it. They spend less time and money on taking care of material possessions, and they have more time and money for things that have lasting value to them.

63.

Assess the Museum

It is both a joy and sadness to most of us that where there's life, there's change. The various phases and cycles of life add great variety and surprise to our existence. They also show themselves in creeping decay. You may relish every minute of this ever-changing life, or you may regret the relentless way that it marches on. The wise person at least recognizes the inevitability of change and makes some kind of peace with it.

Your home almost certainly reflects the many changes of life. At the most basic level, you can see the wear and tear that time exerts on all physical things. Paint peels, fabrics wear, wood accumulates scratches and watermarks, and fragile belongings crack or break. Upkeep is an important element of housecleaning, but you can miss the need for it in the day-in, day-out activities of life.

This is true, as well, in regard to several of your possessions. Just as things suffer the physical ravages of time, they can outlive their usefulness or relevance. You keep them because you've had them forever. You forget to stop and think whether you still want or need them.

Make a yearly habit of assessing what you have accumulated in your home. Look at everything with as fresh an eye as you can. If it helps, imagine that you have an auspicious guest due to visit. Think of how your home would appear to a stranger who does not know you and is unfamiliar with your place. What would you want to spruce up? What would you suddenly realize has been in exactly that place, virtually unnoticed, for the past decade? What would you want to hide?

This exercise is not designed to make you feel self-conscious or inadequate. Everyone needs a fresh take on their surroundings from time to time. If you make assessment a regular habit, you'll probably find it easier to stay on top of maintenance jobs. You may also have an easier time divesting yourself of objects that have lost their original meaning or purpose in your life. Your reward will be a home that truly represents who you are today.

64.

Furnish for Cleanliness

Placement of furnishings certainly affects your ability to clean house efficiently. Just as important are the materials and durability of the things that you choose for your home. The darker the surface, the more dust that it shows; the lighter the surface, the greater effect that smudges will have. The more textured the surface, the more dirt that it holds, and the more fragile the surface, the more damage the soil does.

Consider carefully the sorts of fabrics and finishes that you decide to use in your home. Count the cost when you make selections that will need a lot of maintenance to look good. A stucco wall surface will be harder to wash. A white carpet will show every tiny spot and be unforgiving when a stain is stubborn. A silk-covered chair will not only wear more readily, it will take special care to clean it.

Think, too, about the finishes that you use. Coffee tables in a hospitable home see a lot of beverage glasses and hors d'oeuvres.

Unless you use a waterproof finish, you'll probably have your work cut out for you removing rings and blemishes. Any tables on which you keep living plants will probably take some water abuse, as well. Painted wood furniture that gets a lot of use may need touch-ups more often than furniture with natural finishes, due to chipping. Work surfaces will serve you best if they can be washed with soap and water regularly.

Practicality versus style is one of the perennial tensions in home decorating. If a clean, lustrous look appeals to you, you have to reckon with life as it's lived in your house. The elegant homes of the wealthy may look spotless to the outside observer—in fact, they may be spotless. What you don't know is how many people it takes to keep them in that condition, and at what cost. If one of your goals is to reduce the amount of work it takes to have a clean, attractive home, then choose furnishings that stand up to everyday use, show the dirt slowly, and clean easily.

65.

Remember the Heights

Since we live in a world governed by the laws of gravity, we expect to find things like dust and dirt below eye level, where it "settles." While gravity certainly has its effect on even the lightest particles afloat in the house, it doesn't send everything to the floor and lower surfaces. When you clean, you need to look up, as well as down.

If you have exposed beams, for example, or other architectural elements with surfaces above eye level, remember that the upper surfaces that you can't see catch dust just as surely as the top of a dresser. Because those high surfaces are rarely, if ever, disturbed and even seen, you can get away with neglecting them for quite a spell. At least a couple of times a year, however, remember that dust awaits in those high spots. Hardware stores and cleaning supply outlets sell dusting tools with extension capabilities that will allow you to reach the heights. If you choose to climb a ladder, just make sure that you have a spotter.

Wall fixtures, chandeliers, and the top edges of your woodwork also need attention. These, too, can wait longer than visible surfaces.

Just keep in mind that lighting fixtures will eventually begin to look dingy, and dust film that mixes with oily substances in the air will turn recalcitrant. A simple dusting wand makes dusting such items a breeze. Once or twice a month, start your dusting with a quick swipe over all of the upper surfaces, and you'll be in good shape.

Finally, don't forget the "lace curtains" that accumulate as if by magic in the upper corners, along the ceiling, and on the surface of the walls. Web-builders make their nests and traps in those spots, and the webs in turn collect tiny airborne particles. Nothing detracts from the appearance of spit-and-polish quite like a dangling web. These are easy to spot and wipe away, as long as you are looking for them.

Cleaning has its ups and downs. Start with the ups and move on to the downs. With a little bit of awareness and only light effort, you can keep your home clean from top to bottom.

66.

Use a Flashlight

Why stay in the dark about dirt that lurks in out-of-the-way places? A pocket flashlight can help you stay aware of what's collecting in the dim corners at the back of your closets, behind the furnace, under the sink, and in the coils of the refrigerator. As with other hidden dirt, the dust and grime in these places may not be visible, but it contributes to your workload in other places.

Closets make ideal breeding grounds for mold and mildew. Not only can these growths wreak havoc on your shoes and clothes, they cause many people allergy woes. Unless you take steps regularly to keep the mold and mildew under control, you'll see damage to paint, as well. Take the flashlight to the back of your closets regularly. When dust collects, give the space a quick vacuum. At the first sign of mildew, use a good solution of mold and mildew killer. It's not a bad idea to use mildew-resistant paint in such places. A dish of dehumidifying crystals may help, as well.

The space under the sink can also breed mildew, whether in the kitchen, bathroom, or utility room. Any dampness there will not only contribute to the growth of mold and mildew, it will create a distinctly unpleasant odor over time. Keep an eye out for signs of trouble and deal with them promptly.

The dust and grime that gathers around furnaces, water heaters, and refrigerators needs to be addressed from time to time for more than one reason. Like other hidden dirt, it can be wafted into general circulation if it isn't cleaned up. It may also affect the efficiency and operating life of the parts that it coats. Many refrigerators come with a removable grill over any coils beneath or behind the appliance specifically so that you can run the dust nozzle of the vacuum over them.

It never hurts to shed a little light on a subject. Use a simple penlight or a standard household flashlight to see where you stand on hidden dirt.

67.

Be Generous

Generosity—giving liberally—has a way of making us feel rich, whether in material goods or in spiritual dimensions. We give out of some abundance of our own, which reminds us that we are blessed. Generosity has its visible results in the specific ways that we give of ourselves and our substance, but it starts with an attitude of kindness and openhandedness.

What does this have to do with housecleaning? We commonly view housecleaning as a chore, and because of that, we dread it, resent it, seek to avoid it, and want to be through with it. However, any job that you do, housecleaning included, that aims to make life better for you and yours is, by definition, a generous act. You give of your time, physical strength, creativity, and money to keep your house clean and neat. You share the good results with the people who live with you and the guests that you invite in.

Generosity is rarely understood or appreciated in equal measure to what it costs. For that reason, the wise people of the ages have counseled against doing good for the gain that you'll receive. True generosity is unconditional, extended out of a good heart and a will to share.

Consider the housework that you do as a gift you offer to those that you care about. Far from being a thankless, meaningless cycle of repetitive work that makes your back ache and nose get stuffy, view it as a steady, life-enhancing way of showing love and comradeship. It takes a big person to do things for others, especially when there's no glory or honor in doing them. Yet, isn't such giving of self exactly what love and fellow feeling is all about? The so-called menial work of life is just as important as the jobs that get the big paychecks and the pats on the back. Be generous in your housecleaning. Consider it a worthy job for the sake of a higher quality of life.

68.

Think One Space at a Time

If your house and the work that it takes to keep it up leave you dazed and confused from time to time, try looking at them from a new point of view. Most jobs need to be broken down into their component parts sooner or later. No one can do everything at once. This is just as true of your housecleaning as it is of any other job.

Probably the most effective way to neutralize the paralyzing feelings of having too much to do around the house is to choose a single space at a time for your attention. Focus on one room—perhaps the room in which you spend the most time, or the room to which you retreat when you want to rest. Make it your immediate project to bring that single room to a state of glowing, dirt-free beauty. Give it your all, doing both regular and occasional jobs and addressing the minor repairs and touch-ups that wear and tear require. If there are organizational improvements needed, put them into action, deciding what belongs in the space and what doesn't, and making sure you've provided for the storage that you want.

Don't stop until the room gleams and you can't think of another thing to do. Then move on to another space.

Such an approach has the advantage of helping you accomplish more than the minimum removal of dirt. As you clean, you create lasting improvements that will simplify your cleaning in the future and encourage you to keep the room in such good condition. You also gain the immense satisfaction of having done something completely and with excellence.

As you continue through your house with this intense approach, you're likely to see more clearly which rooms and spaces warrant a lot of attention and which don't. As you weed out the important from the minor, that sense of being overwhelmed will subside, once and for all. You'll be able to face the task of keeping your house in good order with the sure knowledge that you're in control.

69.

Remember to Rest

Working yourself into a state of exhaustion leaves you with resources depleted and spirits lagging. It also creates a mindset of dread for the next time that you have to do the work. The entire enterprise swells to monstrous proportions in your thinking, so that you feel tired before you start.

Understand and honor your own limits. If you have particular physical issues, take them into account. For example, an allergy to dust or mold may make cleaning more tiring for you than for someone else who doesn't suffer the allergic reactions. You may want to help yourself out with a mild allergy inhibitor or a face mask such as is sold inexpensively at drugstores and hardware stores.

Pay attention to such challenges as knee, elbow, or back maladies. Cleaning potentially includes plenty of kneeling, bending, twisting, and lifting. If any of these motions aggravate your body parts, look for smarter ways to work, or delegate the jobs that you really ought to avoid to another member of your household. Take full advantage of any braces or supports that your doctor may have recommended. Housework is hard work and should be respected as such.

Even if you have no restrictions or special considerations to keep in mind, remember that injuries often happen when you push yourself beyond reasonable limits. Don't make the mistake of becoming a martyr to your housecleaning. When you start to flag, take a break, even it's a short one. Sit down and have a snack or a cup of tea. Step outside for a few minutes of fresh air and sunshine. Then get back to work.

If something starts to really ache or hurt, listen to this important message from your body. It may be the first signal that you are using a body part too hard or in a potentially damaging position. It takes much less time to avoid an injury than it does to heal it. When in doubt, stop the action. Move to a different activity or call a halt altogether until you know what's what.

Housecleaning can be a big job. Treat it as such by pacing yourself and resting when you need to. Better to leave some dust than to collapse in clean quarters.

70.
Add Pleasure to Pain

Okay, so maybe there isn't a pep talk or word of encouragement in the world that will coax you into seeing housecleaning as anything but a big old pain in the neck. It's tedious, unending, and totally lacking in glory. You view it, at best, as a necessary evil in your life. So treat it as the nasty medicine it is by adding the proverbial "spoonful of sugar" to the process. If you can't like housecleaning, at least coat it in candy to make it go down more easily.

Do you enjoy music? Blast it from the stereo while you do your housework. If music doesn't do it for you, choose a book on tape or CD to listen to while you work. Get so lost in the story that you're sorry when the cleaning is done and you have to put the book on hold. You can also listen to instructional CDs on your subject of choice. Study a second language. Learn about a foreign land. Explore the wonders of your own psyche with one of the countless self-help books that have been recorded as audio books.

If you get a kick out of making your home beautiful—but fail to equate that with the cleaning process—make a point of incorporating some decorating work with the cleaning. When you're ready to attack a room, consider moving the furniture around a little. This serves the double purpose of exposing hard-to-reach areas for cleaning and perking up your environment with a change of arrangement. When you reach a room where you like to keep fresh flowers, include the removal of flowers past their prime. As soon as the room is clean, reward yourself with a moment of arranging fresh flowers and placing them on a freshly polished surface.

If you live with the love of your life, share the cleaning with him or her. Make it a joint project that allows you to spend more time together accomplishing something for your mutual benefit. Be sure to throw in a little fun and games while you're at it. You may learn to really love cleaning day.

It doesn't matter what gives you pleasure. You can find simple ways to incorporate it into the mundane business of cleaning your house. It takes only a little imagination and a will to like where you are and what you're doing.

71.

End the Day Well

Cleaning can seem endless and unfulfilling because of how quickly it needs to be repeated. However, keep in mind that there is a time when the cleaning is fresh and the results obvious. How often do you take some moments to appreciate a job well done?

Try planning to end a cleaning day with an evening in. Order your favorite takeout food, light the candles, and simply enjoy the shine that you've given your home. Be where you are, fully aware of your surroundings—their fresh smell and bright surfaces. Take full note of the transformation that you've created.

Think, too, about ways to reward yourself for a job well done. Eat out, order in, or let someone else do the cooking for a change. If you enjoy nothing better than heading for the local theater (or the local video store) and the latest film, make it a habit to follow cleaning day with movie night.

Some of the greatest pleasures of housecleaning occur in its immediate aftermath. Don't be in such a hurry to move on to the next thing that you fail to appreciate what you've just accomplished.

72.

Start the Day Fresh

Cleaning takes energy of all sorts. It can be physically taxing, to be sure. It can also call on your spiritual and emotional resources to do it well and with a good attitude.

Understand that your sense of well-being depends in part on how you care for your physical needs. A lack of adequate sleep or poor eating habits can have a significant effect on everything you do. If you want to enjoy what you're doing and have the wherewithal to do it well, you need to take care of yourself.

Give yourself the benefit of rest and perspective when you approach a big cleaning job or a whole-house cleaning day. Trying to do the big stuff when you've already worn yourself out with a day's business or a strenuous physical workout may be stacking the deck against yourself. Treat housecleaning as the physical activity it is, and prepare for it.

First and foremost, plan to get a good night's rest and eat a healthy breakfast. Both are essentials for operating at your optimum, no matter what you're up to. If possible, do your heavy cleaning at the time of day when you're most energetic. It will feel less onerous and go faster when you're at your perkiest. Save the light work for the times when your energy and enthusiasm are sinking.

Remember, too, that it's all too easy to drag a lot of excess baggage around from one day to the next. Regrets about what you failed to accomplish yesterday can sit on your chest like a lead weight when it's time to start today. Whatever happened yesterday, and whatever you have or have not done, today is a new day. You can make this day your starting point, because in reality, that's exactly what it is. Let go of past disappointments and discouragement. Recognize that what you choose today is what matters. Assess where you are and what you hope to accomplish, and create a plan that is based on today's opportunities, not on yesterday's shortcomings.

73.

Shorten the List

It's hard to get excited about a project that looks like the Loch Ness monster in proportion. A "to do" list that rattles on for page after page or a refrigerator door that's plastered with cleaning notes can really sink your spirits. If you tend to really load the "home" work on yourself, you might want to try some different motivational strategies for getting the work done.

To begin, scrutinize your list. Are there any items listed that have already been handled? If so, give yourself the satisfaction of drawing a firm, dark line through them. Are there items that are actually duplicated under a different name? Scratch them, too. Keep at it until you can say with assurance that everything on the list belongs there.

Next, look for any items that you can do in fifteen minutes or less. Assign a specific date to each one, preferably within the coming week, and make a point of doing at least one of them right away. This is a quick, legitimate way of shortening the list in a hurry and clearing the decks for jobs that will be more involved.

Once you've pared your list down to the bigger jobs waiting for action, scan the items to find the one that deserves first attention. Put a star next to it, and figure out exactly when you'll have time to tackle it. Make a date with yourself to do it at that time. The minute that it's done, cross it off the list.

Almost certainly, more cleaning jobs will occur to you before you're finished with the list at hand. If any of them fall into the fifteen-minute-or-less category, knock them off as soon as possible. You can always find fifteen minutes if you really want to. In the meantime, add the other items to the running list, but never let a list run over onto a second page. Make sure that you continue to practice list-shortening techniques. Make your mountain a molehill, and keep it that way.

74.

Get Out of the House

Sometimes, when faced with housecleaning, the best thing you can do is just knuckle down and get the job done. However, never feel obligated to plow ahead, no matter what. In the arena of housecleaning, it's never a matter of life and death. Your physical well-being and mental health definitely rate higher on the importance scale than waxing the floor or cleaning the oven. In fact, no cleaning job should be elevated to such importance that it has the ability to rob you of needed rest or recreation.

When you need to take a time-out, take it. For the sake of fresh air and perspective, get out of the house altogether. Take a walk. Run an errand. Work in the garden for a while. Focus your attention outside your own four walls long enough to restore your essential good humor and sense of proportion. Much larger issues loom in the world—and far greater delights beckon. Leave the housecleaning behind for a bit. You'll be far better equipped to tackle it when you've been away from it for a while.

75.

Give Laundry Lessons

Many families depend on one family member to do all or most of the household laundry. This approach does allow for some efficiencies of scale, but it can also unfairly burden one person while absolving the rest from all responsibility. Since everyone helps to make the dirty laundry, it's not such a stretch to think that everyone can lend a hand when it's time to do the laundry.

Spouses and partners have their own ways of working out the logistics. If one person is content to do the work, that's fine, but there are plenty of ways to divvy it up so that both contribute. At the least, each person should make sure that his or her own dirty clothes find their way to the hamper or laundry room. It's nonsense for anyone in this day and age to throw dirty garments on the floor and expect someone else to pick them up. It takes no more effort to put soiled laundry where it belongs than to let it drop.

Laundry and ironing can be jobs that are traded off or assigned to separate individuals. The non-laundry person can take responsibility for folding his or her own clean clothes fresh out of the dryer, or can be in charge of sorting, folding, and putting away socks. Any way that one person can ease the work of the other makes the job less discouraging.

Parents should think in terms of training their children to be involved in laundry from an early age. As soon as children are old enough to walk, they can put clothes in the hamper. By the time that they're dressing themselves, they can be involved in carrying their folded laundry to their rooms or even putting the clothes away. By adolescence, they should be sharing the job with the adults in the house in one way or another. Whether they have to do the whole job for the family once in a while or just take care of their own clothes, they need to get involved. Knowing how to do your own wash is a valuable life skill.

One last suggestion: When your children at college come home for holidays and summers, don't let them dump their wash back in your lap. They're old enough to take care of themselves.

76.

Practice Laundry Efficiency

It may seem that throwing a few items in the wash every morning saves you a big job at the end of the week. On the other hand, you may feel that the more you can cram into the machine, the better. In fact, the most efficient way to use your washer and dryer almost always falls between these two extremes.

Smaller-than-capacity loads take as much running time and use nearly as much water and electricity, even with "water saver" options, as full loads. In environmental terms, this equals an unnecessary waste of both water and power. While many people in the United States have never experienced a shortage of either, experts predict that the time will come when we will all run short. In the meantime, conservation efforts serve the best interests of the community, regardless of the perceived abundance.

Larger-than-capacity loads may appear to save time and resources, but in fact, they do far more harm than good. Overloading a washing machine puts a strain on the motor and the parts. That's one of the reasons why the manufacturer specifies what constitutes a full load. Because the clothes cannot move freely in the agitation cycles, they don't receive the full benefit of the cleaning agent or the spin cycle. With more water in them, they need additional dryer time, which of course—because the dryer includes a heating element—can use a significantly greater amount of electricity. Furthermore, the extra baggage in the dryer means, again, cramped quarters. By the time that you unload your clothes, you face a load of wrinkles that infect even the permanent press items. That, in turn, means more time and electricity because you have to iron.

Your best bet is to do laundry when you have a full load. Clothes will look their best if you separate lights and darks, and those with special fabric requirements. They'll also get the kindest treatment that your machine has to offer, because you're using the machine as it was designed to be used. If you do a full load as soon as you have one, and fold or hang the clothes promptly, you'll never face a mountain of clean wash waiting to be handled, and you'll probably have next to no ironing.

77.

Be Prompt

Procrastination is a hard habit to break, but it's probably one of the single most controllable sources of stress in modern life. Every time that you see something that needs to be done and choose to put it off, you introduce a little prickle-point into your psyche. Put enough jobs off, and you travel around with a veritable porcupine of worry in your head. Let's face it. Life is stressful enough without adding an extra, unnecessary source. Habits can be broken just as surely as they are formed, and procrastination is nothing more than that—a habit.

Start with the small, daily chores. Make your bed as soon as you rise. Do the dishes as soon as a meal is over. Sort and read through your mail as soon as you retrieve it from the mailbox. Hang up your clothes as soon as you remove them.

Overcoming procrastination in relation to the small things will give you a huge leg up when it comes to dealing with the big things. For starters, you won't have all of those daily issues niggling at your consciousness, and that will free up both your thought and your time. Furthermore, you'll have gained both experience and satisfaction in dealing with jobs as soon as they need doing. The more that you experience the release from stress that attends prompt action, the more that you'll crave it.

For the big jobs that you habitually postpone, sit down and make a plan. Figure out exactly how much time and what supplies you'll need to do a particular job. Be realistic! Underestimating the job will only lead to frustration, half-finished work, and further procrastination in the future. Once you've figured out what the job will take, get it on your calendar. Make it as firm a date with yourself as you'd make another event with a friend. Make sure that you plan a time, as well, for any advance work, such as shopping, that needs to be done before the larger job can be accomplished. Then, when the date arrives, put your plan into action.

This may sound like overkill for a simple housecleaning chore, but the fact remains that many people never catch up with housework and suffer endless stress over that reality for sheer lack of a plan to do otherwise. Procrastination has few, if any, good results. Dump the habit once and for all.

78.
Spot-Clean

There's more than one definition of "spot-cleaning," and they're all relevant to making your housecleaning easier, less stressful, and more rewarding. You don't have to perennially face big jobs when you clean. With a little attention and even less elbow grease, you can stay ahead of the game.

The most common understanding of spot-cleaning is that you clean just the spot that is dirty, rather than tackling an entire area or piece of furniture. In other words, if one of the kids let an open-faced peanut-butter sandwich fall facedown on the living room sofa, you don't call a cleaning service to steam-clean the whole thing. You simply clean up the soiled spot. The net result is that the whole item—whether it's the floor, a counter, a piece of furniture, or the wall—looks relatively good between the necessary overall cleanings it gets. This is a good, commonsense definition that represents a good, commonsense way of handling household cleaning. Apply it to your oven and range, your clothes, your table and bed linens, your doors and door frames, and anything else that is vulnerable to spot dirt.

Here's another simple way to understand the idea of spot-cleaning. When you spot it, clean it. In other words, strike while the iron is hot. Take care of it sooner rather than later, while it's in your range of vision and before you forget about it. The basic result pertains, no matter how you understand the concept. By taking care of small cleaning needs while they're still small, you avoid unwieldy amounts of extra work when the big cleaning jobs come due. Because you've stayed on top of the spills, smears, prints, and stains, you don't have a lot of minutiae to tack onto the overall work.

The small jobs add up in a hurry when you ignore them. Save yourself future steps and strain by handling them right away.

79.

The Art of a Lick-and-a-Promise

Sometimes, you simply do not have the time to do everything to the utmost. At such moments, it pays to have a clear sense of which efforts will pay the greatest dividends. In other words, if you have to do a halfway job on your cleaning, you need to decide which half to leave undone.

Some commonsense do's and don'ts pertain here. For example, do include any job that has an impact on how fresh and clean your house smells—change the cat's litter, empty ashtrays, give the bathroom a once-over, relieve the refrigerator of any food that has gone bad, and install a fresh box of baking soda. On the other hand, don't run a dust cloth along the outer edges of tabletops and other surfaces while leaving knickknacks and lamps in place; an undusted surface actually appears cleaner than one on which you can see the contrast of dusted and undusted areas.

Your lick-and-a-promise job should always include the high-traffic areas—kitchen, entryway, doormats, and floors in high-activity rooms. If you're preparing to entertain, concentrate all of your efforts on the areas that your guests will see, and leave the private quarters for another day. Simply close the doors to those rooms until your guests leave. As far as they'll know, your whole house is as pristine as the rooms in which you entertain.

If you're about to have overnight guests, spruce up the guest quarters to the limit. Put fresh flowers on the dresser of your guestroom. Toss your guest towels into the dryer to give them a freshly fluffed feel. Air the bed linens outside, if you can, for that wonderful outdoor smell. Your guests will remember your royal treatment of them far more than whether every room in the house was just so.

If it's just one of those weeks when your time has gotten away from you, concentrate on the basics. Sanitize, de-clutter, and de-grit. Even the dusting can wait a week. Just make your house tidy and sanitary enough to be livable, and leave the rest for next time.

80.

Observe Others

People come from a wide variety of backgrounds and experiences, and this can show up even in the realm of housecleaning. Different upbringings produce different comfort levels with clutter and dirt, so what one person might consider indispensable, another thinks of as trivial. It's good to keep this in mind when you're stressing out over the state of your house. There's a very good possibility that others simply don't see your house the way you do.

When you visit others, informally or otherwise, take note of the way that people keep house. You're bound to encounter both people who work much harder at keeping their house spotless than you do and those who seem to have a much more nonchalant attitude toward the whole enterprise. Ask yourself: When I visit, am I distracted by the level of cleanliness, whether it's obsessive, slovenly, or something in the middle? Do I think less or more of this person because of the condition of his or her home? Does the way that this person keeps house have anything to do with how welcome I feel?

Keep in mind that the preceding questions have no right or wrong answers. They simply help you understand what matters to you and why. They may also serve to broaden your perspective on the subject of housecleaning. As children, we often conceive the notion that the way that our parents do things is the right way. Then, beginning in adolescence, we spend the rest of our lives trying to shed that conviction so that we can live comfortably in our own skins. You can facilitate that process by putting yourself in other people's environments and seeing how their life choices differ from your own.

The more that you observe, the more that you'll hone your own sense of what matters. Feed this learning curve, and honor it. No matter where you fall in the spectrum, you will live with the least amount of stress when you know yourself and live true to who you are and what you value.

81.

Get Help

There's no shame in doing your own housecleaning—but neither is there any dishonor in hiring help if you can afford it and feel that you need it. Certainly, for households in which all of the adult members have full-time occupations outside of the house, using up those precious few hours away from work on housecleaning can feel like a low blow. If no one in your household stays home full-time, you may want to consider freeing up some of your cleaning time by hiring someone to help.

Start by getting the straight scoop on what individuals or services are available in your area and what they cost. Keep in mind that you don't have to make it an all-or-nothing deal. You can have someone help daily, once a week, every other week, once a month, seasonally, or for certain specific big jobs.

Once you've determined what the possibilities are, look at your budget. Do you have the discretionary funds to hire someone, even if it's just on a limited basis? If not, are there ways that you presently allocate funds that could be shifted to allow some cleaning money? Keep in mind that your time is worth money, as well. What do you earn an hour, approximately, after taxes? Lay that figure alongside what you would pay for an hour of cleaning help. Is it worth it?

Of course, even if you have no interest in hiring help under normal circumstances, you may find times in your life when it's the difference between misery and comfort. When you face an unusually heavy work schedule for an extended period of time, when you bring a new baby home from the hospital, when you are injured, ill, or hospitalized, or even when a big event such as a wedding is in the works—at these or other extraordinary times, some backup on the housecleaning can be more than welcome.

Hired help is not for everyone, but sometimes it can make a huge difference in the quality and workability of your life. In any event, it is a readily available option that you may want to tuck into your back pocket.

82.

The Therapeutic Value of Cleaning

Housecleaning, while creative in its own ways, has a lot of repetitive work in it. For that reason, it can take on a mechanical rhythm that many people actually find soothing. Alternatively, housecleaning can provide a positive and productive outlet for pent-up emotions. Anger, frustration, and anxiety can all do a job on your physical well-being if they go too long unexpressed. While the ideal expression is sometimes dealing directly with the source of the emotion, there are many times when you simply don't have that option available.

When you're in a stew, try taking it out on the dust and grime in your house. Push the vacuum, scrub the floor, or whirl through the house with a clothes basket and pick up every last item that's out of place. Wear yourself and your emotions out doing something that gives you some satisfaction on the other end. Housecleaning probably won't cure your problems, but it can provide a little therapy in the meantime.

83.

Do It for You

Unfortunately, it's the rare person who actually hears, "Well done and thanks so much," at the end of the cleaning day. Rather, we no sooner stow the cleaning supplies than someone is traipsing in with mud on his or her boots, someone else is making crumbs in the kitchen, and yet another one is hot on our tired heels, making demands. Sound familiar?

Don't let it get you down. Some jobs seem predestined to go relatively unnoticed. As nice as it would be to receive all of the kudos that we deserve, it just doesn't happen very often. Rather than letting the reality throw you into a tantrum or the blues, give it a different twist in your own thinking, one that gives you some of the satisfaction that goes begging when the praise is handed out.

Let's grant that at least some of the cleaning that you do was made necessary by the mess that other people made. Concede, as well, that one of the reasons that you want a clean house is to make it nice for others. At the same time, isn't there a real sense in which the person that you clean your house for the most is yourself?

If you answered no, rethink the housework that you're choosing to do. It is beyond thankless to wear yourself out meeting a standard to which you don't subscribe. If you're doing the work, follow a standard that makes sense to you. If someone else in the household wants more, invite them to pitch in and bring the finished product to a level that makes them happy.

If you're honest, you'll probably admit that you find the motivation for the housecleaning in your own preferences. You do it because you enjoy the result. You do it because it makes a difference to your quality of life. There's nothing wrong, nothing selfish or egotistical, in making yourself the one that you hope most to please. Notice your own good efforts and appreciate what you accomplish. Give yourself a good pat on the back and be thankful that you have the strength and know-how to do what you do.

84.

Hold the Line

Sometimes, even with the best intentions, we find it hard to accomplish all that we hope to do. That list of cleaning chores never seems to shorten, and when we look around, the undone jobs scream at us for attention. Our spirits sink, inertia creeps in, and suddenly the list is actually growing. Succumbing to such feelings over any length of time generally results in self-sabotage. We don't scold ourselves into greater energy or productivity. We defeat our good intentions with negativity.

When you find yourself slipping, create a strategy. Assess where you are at the moment. What's keeping you from getting to or completing the housecleaning that you need to do? What exactly needs to be done, and when? What do you need in order to get started?

Once you've assessed, build a plan of action. Don't let the fact that you can't do everything stop you from doing something. Okay, so maybe you can't make any substantial progress on the house in the near future. You can certainly try to keep it from falling into deeper need.

Commit yourself to some reasonable amount of time and effort each day. Don't shoot for the stars. You'll only heighten your sense of inadequate performance. Instead, promise to invest, say, a half hour in housework a day. Nothing more than that. When you've finished your half hour, release yourself from the business for the rest of the day and get on to other things without house-related guilt. If you can manage more, commit yourself to more. If you get into a groove and want to keep going, keep going—but let yourself off the guilt hook the minute you've fulfilled the promise that you made.

Doing a little every day helps you hold the line against the downward spiral. It takes some pluck to put the plan into action, but it can reverse the negative momentum until you get back into a more effective routine. Some of the most debilitating energy in our lives comes from inside our own heads. Instead of tearing yourself down for what you haven't done, become your own source of encouragement for what you will do from now on.

85.

Know When to Quit

Is enough ever enough for you when it comes to cleaning? Many people suffer from a need to achieve. They want to be perfect. They deeply fear failure. They have a low sense of self. As a result, they live in a state of extreme imbalance that precludes play and pleasure and a well-rounded diet of activities that can sustain and inspire them.

Because of its nature—with results that never last long—housecleaning can feed the worst instincts of the classic overachiever. A house is rarely or ever in an actual state of perfect cleanliness. One could conceivably give the best part of every day to striving for such a condition, but to what good end? Housecleaning is just one of many facets of the average person's life. It's necessary. It's worthwhile. But it's not everything.

When you decide what needs to be done around your house, remember to keep housecleaning in balance with the rest of your life. It's easy to tell your teenage children that you need to finish the dishes before you discuss their problems, but it may be that now is the moment when your children want and need your undivided attention. The dishes will definitely be there when you return from a heart-to-heart discussion. Your children may not be available or open by the time that you finish cleaning up the kitchen.

So, too, on that perfect first day of spring, when the air turns balmy and the birds fill the sky with song. Will you turn down a friend's invitation to take a walk together so that you can finish scrubbing the shower walls, or will you give yourself a heart-lifting break in the fresh air and sunshine, knowing that a quick rinse of the shower will allow you to leave the work till another time?

It's so easy, when you're on a cleaning mission, to forget that the quality of your life depends on feeding all of the aspects of your being. Sometimes, it may be better to have a dirtier house for the sake of a better life. Give yourself permission to quit the cleaning when other, more balancing activities intrude.

86.

Take Care of Little Things

Have you ever heard the expression, "Take care of the pennies, and the dollars will take care of themselves"? While the expression sounds anachronistic—pennies aren't what they used to be—the sentiment remains true. When we disrespect little things, we shortchange the larger issues that they add up to. When we pay consistent attention to the details, the overall picture brightens.

Chances are that you don't jot down every last little job that goes into keeping everything neat and clean when you make your "to do" list—nor should you. However, don't let the fact that some activities are too minor to list keep you from giving those minor jobs their due. Staying on top of the little jobs adds up to making the big jobs a lot less onerous and less frequent.

Carry a hand towel around with you when you water plants, and wipe up those inevitable drips before they have a chance to mar the finish on a wooden surface. Keep the coasters handy and use them when you carry cups or glasses out of the kitchen. Give yourself a little bend-and-stretch exercise by picking up visible lint, stones, or bits of food when you see them on the floor. Wipe the smudge off the cabinet or door while it's still fresh.

When you see something simple that ought to be attended to— a cobweb in the corner, a ridge of dust that you missed, or a picture out of kilter on the wall—take the thirty seconds or less that is required to fix it. For little things, there's almost always no time like the present. All you need is an observant eye and a ready hand.

Think of such trivial actions as an investment in your larger housecleaning efforts. Imagine that you have a house-shaped piggy bank, and every small effort is a coin dropped in the slot. It really adds up over the long haul, and it takes so little at the moment.

87.

Replace Bad Tools

People operate from a wide variety of philosophies when it comes to buying cleaning supplies and tools. Some folks are determined to find a bargain. Others are always on the lookout for the next glitzy product on the market. Some people would sooner shop for anything than a cleaning tool. Others can't seem to buy enough.

Let common sense be your guide when you consider cleaning tools. If the vacuum, mop, dust cloth, or squeegee that you have now is getting the job done to your satisfaction, there's no reason to fix what isn't broken. However, cleaning instruments are subject to all of the laws of depreciation and decay at work on the rest of the material world. They wear out, break, and otherwise fall into a state of decline. You don't have to wait until the situation is dire before you look into updating your tools.

If you have any tools that really should be replaced, think in terms of replacing them with the best quality that you can afford. Do your homework. Find out what various tools promise and what distinguishes one from another. Consider the actual needs of your household, not just the claims of a particular product. Make full use of consumer services that rate various products and manufacturers and provide point-by-point comparisons of like categories. Choose carefully and with an eye to purchasing a tool that will have the longest life possible.

Once you acquire good tools, keep track of guarantees and warranties. Even fine products sometimes come off the assembly line with flaws. Certain models may have design problems that become apparent only after they've been on the market for some time. You'll feel easier in mind and wallet if you take advantage of replacement and repair promises made by a manufacturer. Within a certain time frame, it's insulting to have additional expenses on a good tool.

Your ultimate goal is to keep your supply closet stocked with quality tools in excellent operating condition. When one of your household helpers has reached the end of its usefulness, treat yourself to the best replacement within your budget.

88.

Enjoy the Ridiculous

Yes, housecleaning can feel like serious business, but like every aspect of life, it contains its share of the absurd and the ridiculous. You can fret and fuss over it, or you can have a sense of humor, and let it go. Laughter is a powerful life skill.

First of all, understand that Murphy's Law has its basis in fact. There are days when anything that can go wrong will go wrong. Generally speaking, these are the days when you're on a tight time frame, you're expecting important company, or you're getting ready to go away and leave the house in someone else's care. No one knows why this law is true. It just is. When one frustration or catastrophe follows another, just chalk it up to one of the fundamental laws of nature, and get on with your life.

Murphy's Law isn't the only principle or tendency at work in your household. The idea that what gets done comes undone—formalized by scientists under the term "entropy"—is easy to prove in any household, often within hours of finishing a cleaning job.

The trend in the universe, apparently, is from order toward disorder. So why should it be any different in your home?

Of course, there are also the unwritten laws that most people know without any scientific seal of authority. For example, pets (especially cats) always spit up the day after you clean and when company's coming. Milk always spills shortly after you have freshly washed and waxed the kitchen floor. The toilet always overflows when the rugs are clean. A rainstorm with high winds and a lot of leaf debris always hits when the exterior surfaces of the windows have just been washed.

If you want to avoid ulcers and tension headaches, it pays to be a homegrown philosopher. Look at life, with all of its laws and realities, with a twinkle in your eye. Hope for the best and accept the ridiculous. Appreciate its value as material for stand-up comedians and humor columnists. Smile, shrug, and do your best.

89.

Reorganize As Needed

Part of taking a philosophical approach to life in general and to housecleaning in particular is the ability to change when change is called for. No matter how well you've organized your household, you will find times when your organization doesn't do it for you. You'll find yourself consistently running out of time, your cleaning schedule will suddenly conflict with the schedules of others in your household, or the logic that you've applied to the order in which you do things will suddenly make no sense to you.

Don't worry about it! No one way of doing things is the only way to do them. Neither is one way necessarily better than others. What you do and how you do it is in your hands. You get to make the rules. When the times call for change, you get to make new ones.

When things go awry, ask yourself what isn't working. Figure out exactly what you want to happen that you don't see happening at the moment. This process can be remarkably similar to what a doctor does when he or she works on a diagnosis. You may have to go through a process of elimination—something like this: Am I cleaning at a time when there are too many distractions? No, that's not it. Have I allowed too little time for the kind of housework that I want to accomplish in this time slot? Not really. Am I doing the steps in the wrong order for the greatest efficiency? Hmm. Maybe so.

Once you've nailed the problem, it remains to find a solution that works for you. Again, you don't have to find the plan for all time. All you need to do is figure out a way to suit where you are at the moment. Be experimental. Try different cleaning methods. Follow different paths through your house. Mix up the times that you clean or the particular jobs you do on particular days. Most of all, try to hold on to your way of doing things with a light hand. Solutions can surface through a process of elimination just as surely as do the problems.

90.
Accept Change

There are few sure things in life, but one of them is certainly change. Where there's life, you will always find change. Age, circumstances, physical health, family, and jobs shift and realign with one another like so many colors in a kaleidoscope. With such changes come varying amounts of busyness, wisdom, strength, distraction, demands on your time, and interests. For many people, change is disconcerting at best, and at worst, terrifying.

Perhaps change frightens people because it tends to have a ripple effect on all of life that's hard to predict. Change can be totally unrelated to something as personal as keeping house and still create after-changes that make your job harder, more complicated, or simply different. It can come from forces beyond your control, yet you have to deal with the consequences nonetheless.

When changes occur in your life that affect your ability to deal with your household, you have two choices. You can resist change, or you can accept it. Resisting usually only leads to stress and frustration.

Digging in your heels doesn't make change go away. It simply postpones your finding a way to deal with it. You may not relish the idea of facing it squarely and searching for creative solutions, but the alternatives will quickly leave you out of touch with your new reality.

The wisdom of the ages has always advocated the acceptance of inevitable change. Resistance saps your energy and binds your will. Acceptance frees you to apply positive energy to moving forward proactively.

The time may come when you have to reckon with the fact that you don't have the time to do what you once did. You may have to face that you are no longer physically capable of what you could do in your youth. You may have to deal with a new partner in life who has different preferences or values from the ones that you've been accustomed to. Or you may have to shoulder full responsibility for a house that you once shared with someone else.

Whatever changes come to you in this life, some of them will involve things beyond your control. Understand that this is true for everyone. Deal with it from a posture of acceptance, and move forward calmly.

91.
Get Real

The world of dreams, of fantasy and "the ideal," is an important one for anybody who wants to face life with optimism and aspirations. We devise our hopes out of what we can imagine as much as from what we experience. We want to transform our lives, to make them better, more satisfying and meaningful. We fuel this desire with a sense of what's possible.

By all means, let yourself dream about your home, as well. Daydreams of the setting that you would love to create are just as valid as visions of the dream vacation, the perfect job, or the ideal mate. Go ahead and fantasize about a gleaming, orderly place that offers rest, invites hospitality, and truly represents you at your best. Envisioning such a reality can help you work toward it with a solid sense of just what your goal is.

Take care, though, that you don't take the ideal so seriously that anything short of it fills you with feelings of failure and inadequacy. We live in an imperfect world, full of traumas, surprises, disappointments, and unexpected bends in the road. We are also surrounded by media images of life as it might be—might be, that is, if life could be manipulated as easily as an ad campaign or a stage set. It's rare that we ever achieve the ideal. Even when our dreams come true, they often turn out to be quite different from what we expected.

Stick with a sense of balance. Alongside your fantasy image of the perfectly groomed and decorated home, remember reality. Make your practical plans, and invite the members of your household to share in them. Do your best with what you have and keep finding ways to improve what you do and how you do it, but don't expect to be the first person in the universe to overcome the ragged stuff of real life and human relationships. Don't punish yourself for being "one of us," ordinary mortals muddling through with a good will. It's okay to be human.

92.

Carpe Momentum

Inertia can work powerfully against our best intentions and desires. The longer we stay in one place, the stronger those root strands become, until forward motion begins to look like more effort than we can muster.

That's why it's a great idea to seize on the days and moments when your energy is high and your motivation is strong. Who knows what might get you going? Maybe the first invigorating whiff of spring is in the air one day, or you simply woke up in a lively mood. Maybe a long-absent friend is traveling through and staying for a few days. Whatever the cause, when you throw your housecleaning into high gear, make the most of it.

This is called momentum. A body in motion tends to stay in motion just as surely as a body at rest resists action. Once you get going, you can depend on the activity itself to carry you on for some distance. You're up, you're moving, and doing one more job or finishing up something that's been waiting suddenly doesn't seem like such a big deal. Where, on another day, you might be tempted to procrastinate or avoid the work, this time you have the oomph that you need.

Momentum can't be bottled one day and then taken as a tonic at some other time. You need to capitalize on it when you're in the midst of it. Watch for the days when you're really "in the groove" and ready to get things done, and grab those days as the great gifts that they are. Let your energy carry you from one job to the next, putting aside your typical expectations of how much you'll do at a time.

Once you're on a roll, you may discover ways to keep the momentum going. Some people find that if, when the day is winding down, they do just a little of the next job, they can more easily pick it up and finish the next day. Just the fact that they've made a start encourages them to do more. Others find that on energetic days, they can make plans more effectively, which in turn helps them to get going the next time that they have a bit of time to do some housework. Whatever you can do to capitalize on momentum will help to stave off inertia, so when it comes, carpe momentum.

93.

Weed Out the Used Up

Consolidating what you own and what you store has a significant impact on your ability to keep a clean, neat house. When you move, redo a closet, or renovate an attic or basement, take full advantage of the resulting shakeup by making it an opportunity to get rid of the excess. Look for broken items that you will never fix, clothes that will never again fit or return to fashion, keepsakes that have lost their meaning, and hand-me-downs that have not proven appealing or useful. For the most part, such things can be thrown away. On occasion, you may know someone who has a use for junk, collects vintage objects, or uses parts for projects. In that case, you may have a ready outlet. However, it's okay to discard things, as well.

Make a regular habit of going through household supplies. Toss the packaging that somehow hung around after its contents were gone. Take stock of the bottles, cans, and boxes of liquids and powders that never get used up. If these are products that you use regularly and you've started a new container, drain the dregs from the old into the new and throw out the empty. If you have leftovers of a product that you simply don't use anymore, either trash it or give it away. Remember, too, to check for expiration dates. Any item that has passed its date should be gotten rid of.

If you save old clothes and shoes for "work" clothes, assess how much you've set aside for this use. Do you really need four ratty pairs of athletic shoes or loafers? Do you actually dirty five old sweatshirts between laundry days? How much variety in old blue jeans do you need from one messy project to the next? These old duds take up valuable storage space, so notice which garments you use often and which end up living at the bottom of the drawer. Save only what you use, and lose the rest.

Keeping up with the used up will not only free up space, it will lighten the psychological load. Those hidden piles of useless materials weigh on you more than you think. Get into the routine of storing only what you'll use. Then enjoy that feeling of lightness that follows.

94.

Make Friends at the Transfer Station

Sometimes, the business of keeping down clutter and debris in and out of the house overwhelms us simply for lack of doing the preliminary legwork. Most residential areas provide weekly or biweekly trash removal, and that makes it easy for you to keep the small trash under control. However, what about the big items that don't fit in the can or bin? What about the detritus that accumulates in the yard?

If you've never done so, take the time to acquaint yourself with all of the services available to you through your town. Acquire the identification that you need for your vehicle in order to use the dump or transfer station. Find out what special categories of rubbish are provided for there and what you have to do to make your dump-bound loads acceptable. You may discover that you can dispose not only of trash, but also leaves, cut-up wood (many towns don't accept grass clippings), hazardous materials, old furniture, recyclables, and white paper trash.

Check to see if there are occasional, special curbside pickups provided by the town, as well. In many locations that experience four seasons, the town will provide a couple of days through the autumn for leaves that are either bagged or in piles for street sweeping. In addition, there may be provisions for taking away Christmas trees, and the town may add extra "trash days" in the hot weather.

If your community is like most today, you have some number of items that are designated for recycling. You may be able to recycle newspapers and glossy magazines, most glass containers, aluminum cans and foil, certain plastics, cardboard beverage cartons, and even corrugated cardboard. If your town sends out a list or a brochure, make sure that you get a copy and put it somewhere ready at hand. Know the regulations and possibilities, and make full use of them.

It may seem like a small matter, but making yourself familiar with the dump or transfer station and all of the disposal opportunities in your area can make a big difference in your week-to-week housecleaning. If you know what you can toss and how to do it, you're a lot less likely to create stashes of old boxes, paper items, leftover hazardous materials, and so forth. Take guesswork and procrastination out of the mix.

95.

Rethink the "Treasures"

There's no question that it's hard to know sometimes whether something is trash or treasure. It's okay to hold on to things that you think you might like to keep for refurbishing, reuse, or just old times' sake. Eventually, though, when the object has been collecting dust for years or moldering in the back of a closet, you may want to rethink its value to you.

If you have belongings that you think your children might "someday" want to have, establish a storage spot with well-marked containers to hold them. Just as soon as your children are truly on their own, start asking what they want. They'll be able either to take the items off your hands or relieve you of guilt about getting rid of them.

If you simply have a hard time deciding what to do with something, make a commitment to store it for just one year. When you do your spring or fall cleaning, tackling some of the less frequent, bigger cleaning jobs, revisit the question and pin yourself down. You may decide to "hold" for a bit yet, or you may be clearer in your mind that you're never going to have a use for the item again.

The trick, ultimately, is to know what you have. It's all too easy to lose track of the things that you put out of sight, especially when you have no current use for them. The more that you accumulate, the less that you remember, and the more the hidden piles grow. Instead, get into a pattern of periodic review. You may have some real treasures that are worth the space and care that they require. You'll make that storage more efficient and probably more secure when you get rid of the stuff that turns out to be trash.

96.

Use It or Lose It

Just as you may be tying up storage and creating extra work by hiding away belongings that you no longer need or use, you may also have such items filling up shelves and collecting dust on bureau tops, desks, bookcases, and counters. It's easy to take for granted the things that you have around you. Unless they're items that you use regularly, you stop noticing them or the clutter and work that they create.

As part of your cleaning, pay close attention to the knickknacks, appliances, photos, candlesticks, books, containers, and other items that sit in view around your house. Are they still of interest or use to you? Do they add to the overall charm or beauty of your home? Do you have other items that need a place and would be better choices?

As you find objects that have lost their original interest or luster, consider whether it's time to replace them. Unlike human beings, you have no obligation to the inanimate things in your life. If they are still in good repair, you can make a quiet gift of them to someone who would better appreciate them. You can take them to a consignment or thrift shop and redeem some monetary value from them. You can also add them to a tag sale or the "white elephant" table at a community fundraiser.

It can be quite rewarding to give new life to an old belonging while freshening up your own décor. Your tastes have surely changed over time, as have your needs and interests. Why not keep your home current and interesting to you? Like moving furniture or repainting a room, such changes can give you a fresh perspective on your life and your home. At the same time, you keep the clutter down and give someone else the chance to enjoy things that no longer serve you.

This is conscious home management. While autopilot helps in some regards, in others it can bog you down. Be aware of what you have surrounded yourself with and whether you still want it. Be ready to send it on its way when its time with you is over.

97.

Be Bold

If we want to improve what we have and how we do things, we need to face change boldly and take control of what we do next. As you assess your home and plan what you need to do to get housecleaning in order, understand that you are engaged in a courageous process. There will certainly be times when you're overwhelmed with all that needs to be done. You'll look at past efforts that failed to produce the results that you wanted and question your worth and abilities. You'll be tempted to take a hopeless view and simply settle for being discouraged. Every time that you fight through such feelings and start again to make changes for the better, you are taking a brave step that can lead to many others.

Beyond the basic business of accepting the need for change and acting on it, however, a bold approach can help you throughout the process of change. The more that you work at dealing with housecleaning as an enterprise worth your full creativity and energy, the more you'll discover that halfway measures may not make enough of a difference to satisfy you.

Imagine, for example, that you've decided to clean out the storage spaces in your home. Now, you can take on those spaces one at a time over the course of a year, filling a single large trash bag every couple of weeks and making a few little trips to the consignment shops here and there. However, maybe it's worth considering a bolder approach. How about renting a Dumpster, taking a week off from work, and doing the deed in one concentrated, ruthless gulp? Tackle it as though you're about to move into an efficiency apartment and can keep only what will comfortably fit. Abandon the soul-searching over every little item, and make a wholesale sweep of the stuff that is clogging the pores of your home. Can you imagine the sense of accomplishment and pleasure on the other side of such a move?

Sometimes, baby steps are all you can manage, but there are moments when the planets line up and the mood is so perfect that you can be bold and accomplish things in a big way. When such moments arise, go for the big changes that will make you sing.

98.

Pass It On Early

You may own items that, while they may not be of much practical use to you, represent a family legacy or an investment that you eventually want your children to have. If you're actively enjoying such items in the meantime, then it makes sense to find ways to incorporate them into your home without undue crowding or excessive cleaning work. Polishing the silver pieces that sit on the dining room sidebar three times a year can actually be a pleasure.

If, on the other hand, you're just hanging on to things in order to pass them along, consider your timing. There are no laws that say you have to wait until you're dying or dead to give the next generation what will finally be theirs anyway. In fact, it can be a pleasure to both the giver and the receiver to hand over heirlooms and keepsakes early. You add richness and a sense of posterity to a younger person's life, and you have the opportunity to actually watch the person use and enjoy what he or she has been given. In the meantime, you're relieved of the care of items that have ceased, in the overall balance of your life, to be worth the effort to you.

You may also own items that could have value to the general public or to an archive or museum. Paintings or objets d'art that you don't have room to display or store or that don't fit your personal style may offer a worthy addition to an institutional collection that handles similar items. Family papers and antique publications of historical interest may be welcomed by the local historical society or public library. Again, if you don't have any particular desire to have these items in your care, requiring cleaning, storing, and protection, you don't have to postpone a donation until the reading of your will. You can arrange to have the items assessed by an expert and gift them now to an appropriate collection.

Passing heirlooms and curios on while you're hale and hearty not only relieves you of their care, it allows you to fully control their disposition. It also offers some tax advantages to you while you still need them. It's a satisfying way to continue the process of paring down while giving pleasure to others.

99.

Learn to Say "No Thanks"

The business of keeping your house in order suffers setbacks and challenges daily. Forget the dirt and mess that reappear with amazing predictability. You also face the arrival of stuff that you don't need and haven't chosen.

When unappealing gifts arrive, you may not want to bluntly respond with, "Can I exchange this?" People can be surprisingly sensitive on the subject of an item that they picked out, no matter how well or how little they know you. In many cases, the package or box in which an item arrives will identify where it was purchased. If you keep the package, it is often possible to take the item back and explain that it was a gift and you want to exchange it. While most stores won't give you cash, they often have a policy of store credit. You can either find something that you actually want, or you can use the credit the next time that you need to give a gift. By the same token, provided that the people in question don't overlap in social circles, you can actually give the original gift to someone else. Just keep it in the pristine condition in which it arrived until a moment presents itself.

You can deal with similar potential frustrations closer to home, as when a member of your extended family decides to pass along items that you don't want. Although there are exceptions to the rule, in general the best approach in such a situation is the direct one. You can speak honestly while maintaining some sensitivity. "This is lovely," you might say, "and I can't tell you how much I appreciate you thinking of me, but I have no way to display it properly," or, "I think there are other family members who would appreciate it so much more." The giver saves face while getting the message that you would prefer that he or she not give you the item.

When dealing with a spouse who has a penchant for loading the house up with excess, you may have to be even more direct. Communicate clearly and consistently about your desires in relation to a clean, uncluttered house. Make plain exactly how important it is to you. Don't expect your partner to read your mind. A solution will probably call for some compromise on both sides. You may have to say yes to some of the items that you wouldn't otherwise acquire. He or she may have to agree to containing such items to a designated, defined space—his or her study, a corner of the garage, or whatever.

Take control of what comes to your space. You can say, "No thanks." In the process, you'll gain freedom and power to make your home what you want it to be.

100.

Rest and Be Thankful

When the day is done, when you've accomplished what you could, remember to take a little breather and appreciate what you have. It's possible to get so caught up in the mission to improve in a big way that you forget to note the small steps of progress along the way. Every effort that you apply to making your home what you want it to be is a worthy one. In the long run, it's the effort more than the outcome that deserves your attention.

Life in general, other people, circumstances, and unexpected events may turn your best ideas and attempts on their heads. On the other hand, what you do is up to you. Whether it works itself out in just the way that you expected is really beside the point. You've done what you could with good intentions.

So take the time regularly to reward your own efforts with some reflection and quiet. When you're all worked out, sit down and rest. Think about what you were physically able to do. Acknowledge your capacity to plan and organize. Be aware that you have put time and energy into a worthy enterprise. Take note of every benefit that you've produced throughout your home. Look around you. Pat yourself on the back.

Then be thankful. So much of what you have and who you are had its origins in sources and forces outside of your control. In many ways, your life and your being are a gift, pure and simple. Every day that you wake up is a gift. Be conscious of the many ways that you've been gifted, and remember to say "Thank you" for every one of them. Life and home are beautiful for those who live in a state of gratitude.